A Passion *for* Parties

A Passion *for* Parties

Carolyne Roehm

AUTHOR OF *AT HOME WITH CAROLYNE ROEHM*

Broadway Books
New York

acknowledgments

I wish to acknowledge the help of my staff for all of their ceaseless efforts on my behalf, especially Rosa Costa, Placido and Margarida de Carvalho, Leila Roxo, Nancy Quantrini, and Vicky Morrel. Special thanks to Doug Turshen and his team, including David Huang, for interpreting my vision and creating a beautiful layout.

As always a big thank you to my friend and photographer Sylvie Becquet for her artistry. To Tara Sgroi, Antonis Achilleos and Stefan Studer for their photographic talent.

A thank-you to my editors, Jennifer Josephy and Donna Bulseco.

Thank you to my agent, Cullen Stanley, for her continued support and sound advice.

To dear Lisa B. Newsom, editor in chief at *Veranda* magazine, for her thoughtful encouragement.

Thank you to Mom, Mittie Ann, and Simon for their loving support and to my many dear friends who have helped me to prepare my parties.

And to my many supporters across the country, whose constant encouragement already has me dreaming about my next book.

A Passion for Parties is dedicated
to my mother, who inspired me to have
a passion for everything.

contents

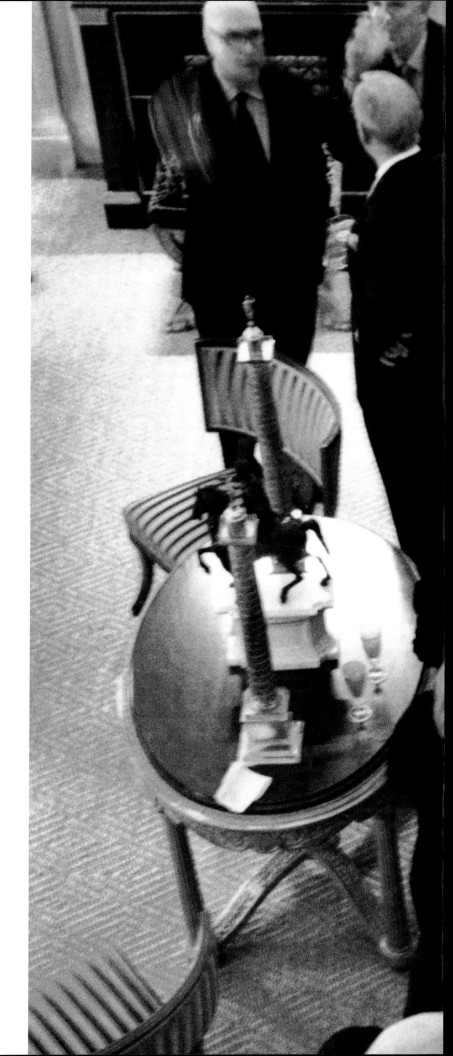

introduction

I have always loved the fantasy of a party. For me, entertaining is one of the most complete expressions of my style as a designer and hostess. Much like creating a dress or a beautiful room, giving a party allows my imagination to venture into a reality that is outside of everyday life. Certainly, I relish the planning that goes into one—choosing an enticing menu, designing the invitations, finding the right decorations, and setting all of the preparations in motion. But for me, it is the initial spark of inspiration that is most thrilling, and it is what prompted me to put together the parties in this book.

Parties define us in many ways, often creating a timeline of our lives and showing how we lived at different moments. We are at our best at a party, suspending our busy lives and shedding our work-crazed selves to adopt the party spirit by donning a costume, doing a do-si-do, or sipping a cocktail. The desire to give life to the kind of fantasy that will evoke an ahhh from my guests tempts me to entertain again and again. You can get that response easily enough—by the flowers you place on a well-set table; the red, white, and blue canopies you hang for a Fourth of July fete; or the jambalaya you prepare for a dinner party.

Taking the time in this fast-paced world to make the effort and create a little magic is incredibly satisfying—no matter how big or small, simple or elaborate the event may be. Many people get hung up on making everything perfect—and I confess that can be a real preoccupation for me, too—but at a certain point, it's best to set things in motion, focus on the key ingredients for a great party (food, drink, a festive environment), and have fun in the creative process. Putting on a party becomes second nature to you once you've done enough of them as I have, so I thought it might be helpful to map out my strategies in the chapter entitled, "The Party Process." It's a checklist of sorts for those who feel they'd like a little help or for seasoned party veterans who like to compare what they do with others. That's another source of satisfaction—you can learn a lot from party-givers, most of all, how to enjoy yourself while you're doing it. Nowadays, I am amazed by how much I rely on my computer and the Internet for my events. How did I do everything before I had these valuable tools? I hope you'll log on to my Web site (carolyneroehm.com) for more information on and help with planning parties, wrapping gifts, and making delicious dishes.

Someday I'm going to do a costume ball, one inspired by the landmark fetes of eighteenth-century France that even now are unrivaled for their creativity, unbelievable food, and spectacular firework displays. That will certainly take a lot of passion to pull off. Until then, I'm more than happy to indulge in littler fantasies.

spring

Spring has always meant new beginnings to me. After being indoors during the long, cold months of winter, the soft breezes and warm temperatures of spring are welcome—and welcoming to guests. It's a season that makes entertaining easy: At the first sign of nice weather, I send out invitations to friends to come over and have lunch by the pool. I'm energized by the fact that I can do the simplest things to great effect, choosing spring's gorgeous blossoms and fresh produce when determining what I'm going to use for decoration and what I'll serve for lunch or dinner. Putting together a party outside allows me to take advantage of what nature brings to the party, so to speak—lush green lawns; peonies in a vast range of pink, fuchsia, and white; tulips; roses; and other fragrant blooms for beautiful arrangements. I'm always inspired by flowers—and I must admit that whenever I see the first spring blossoms at Weatherstone, my Connecticut home, I feel the urge to throw a party to show them off. For a celebration of one of my favorite flowers, peonies, I used masses of them as decorative elements throughout the grounds of Weatherstone, and on tables and trellises. And even when I throw a party indoors—like the children's birthday party shown on the following pages—I am prompted by flowers (in this case, big, vibrant felt ones!) to bring a fun, energetic life to the event. Join me in my homage to spring's infinite beauty.

June peony party

A GARDEN'S WORTH OF EXUBERANT
BLOOMS ENLIVENS A DINNER AND
DANCE OUTSIDE IN THE FRESH SPRING AIR.

Masses of peonies provide a burst of color on a table with rustic linens, blond wood-handled flatware, and glass votives. Guests' names are printed on wooden plant markers used as place cards.

A plain tablecloth and napkins in off-white, beige, or taupe allow the peonies to be the star of the show. I rented fruit-wood ballroom chairs and decorated the backs with variegated ivy runners tied on with raffia bows.

This page: Two tiers of bouquets with mixed peonies and trailing vines of variegated ivy sit below a top tier holding a cluster of votive candles. Opposite page: Terra-cotta pots serve as vases for the extravagant blooms.

A line of iron plant pillars defines the space around the dinner

tables and dance floor, creating the sense of an outdoor room.

The party begins: Cocktails are served in the rose garden, where friends gather to talk about summertime events.

My love for the peonies from my garden inspired me to give a June dance that showcased this glorious flower. Even the names of some of the varieties evoke good times, from the white Festiva Maxima and Marshmallow Puff to the pale pink Moon River and Minuette, to the sultry Champagne and Glowing Raspberry Rose. Armfuls of peonies—some 1,500—were cut mostly in advance, conditioned, and stored in an air-conditioned room, then brought out and arranged in mixed or solid bouquets the morning of the event.

A day in advance, a dance floor was built and stained a soft gray. Iron plant pillars were lined up in a row to define the space, creating the feeling of an outdoor room. Gray garden benches with linen pillows surrounded three sides of the dance floor, so that those who did not want join the action could watch it from the side. Lighting was key in creating a look and a mood. I consider Japanese lanterns a classic and often use them as lighting for a party. At this one, I placed votive candles on little wire platforms inside each lantern, and fastened a fishing line with sinkers so we could string them throughout the maple trees. As it got dark, we lit the candles and raised them up into the branches.

To suit the breezy mood of the party, the dinner menu was light and fresh. The first course of Chilled Fresh Pea Soup with Crab (page 232) was served; then guests helped themselves to a buffet of Poached Salmon with Cucumber Herb Sauce (page 232), fresh spring asparagus from the garden with a bit of lemon butter, and new potatoes with parsley. For those who wanted dessert, there was Angel Food Cake with Coconut Whipped Cream and Strawberries (page 233).

Although I had a DJ and we played a great selection of Motown and disco music, the spirit of the evening was best captured by the ballads of Frank Sinatra. With the white Japanese lanterns swaying overhead and Old Blue Eyes crooning away, the party was as perfect as one of the gorgeous blossoms that inspired it.

All of the neutral shades make a subtle background for

Through the years, I've added more than thirty different varieties to my garden at Weatherstone, which allows me to mix bouquets of different pinks, reds, magentas, and whites. The pots are lined with plastic containers holding Oasis (florist's foam) and a mix of water and flower preservative.

the explosion of color from the lush, fragrant peonies.

I am constantly changing the areas where I set up for a lunch or a big party. I think a new view or unexpected angle on a familiar landscape makes an event more interesting for repeat guests—and it certainly makes it more stimulating for me.

blooms day lunch

AT THE FIRST SIGN OF SPRING, TAKE
ADVANTAGE OF WARMER TEMPERATURES
TO ENTERTAIN OUTDOORS.

Yellow peony tulips and viburnum play off the greens of the English plates and a bowl of Granny Smith apples. These are the last of my tulips to bloom, and I am always amazed at how they are such close cousins to a variety of peony that blooms in mid-June. Rattan chargers and flatware with blond wood handles provide a chic texture to the look of the table.

fter the long New England winter, I can hardly wait to start entertaining outdoors again. During the first warm days of May, I begin to move lunch to the porch and am delighted when we have enough pleasant days in a row to signal the opening of (if not the swimming in) the pool.

It's important to me to change the visual landscape for my parties—even if simply for my own enjoyment! I am constantly mixing up the four sets of dishes and glasses I use outside by the pool, so the arrangements never bore me. One year on my birthday, in early May, my mother gave me a wonderful set of nineteenth-century English leaf dishes I was immediately anxious to use. So a few weeks later, when Mother

Nature came through with a stretch of glorious days, I planned a lunch, and these gorgeous plates inspired a table of green, yellow, and chartreuse. For the centerpiece, I cut a large bouquet of yellow peony tulips from my garden. To play off the luscious green and chartreuse in the plates, I added green viburnum branches to the bouquet. I placed a basket of Granny Smith apples (which I use a lot as an easy and inexpensive decoration because I love the color) on the table to complement the water and wine glasses. Just for fun, I also chose a menu to reflect the palette: Chilled Zucchini Soup with Toasted Coconut (page 234), followed by Yellow Tomato Tartlets (page 234), a frisee and endive salad, and for dessert, a lemon-lime sorbet served in lime shells. Thankfully, the weather was perfect, the light sublime, and the opening days of spring were launched.

I have different sets of pillows and lounge cushions in a variety of hues and patterns that go well with the pool, which is decorated with dark green, blue, and white. All of these colors work beautifully together and create a perfect foil for just about any other shade I want to introduce on my table.

All the elements of the table, including the candy bouquets, party hats, gift-wrapping paper, ribbons, tiny parasols, and oversized throw pillows, are tied together through the use of bright color.

flower power fun

A PARTY FOR CHILDREN SHOULD BRING
OUT THE KID IN YOU, INSPIRING A DOSE
OF WHIMSY AND EFFERVESCENT HUES.

e inventive: Fashion exuberant flowers and lots of

Why not instill the love of parties at an early age? If you create an anticipatory mood, children will sense that something fun and special is about to happen. A festive backdrop and plenty of goodies ensure it will.

polka dots in candy-colored felt to make a bold statement.

Opposite page: Kids love to don party hats, and this one proved irresistible.
This page: Oversized pillows serve dual purposes, providing comfortable seating and an explosion of cheerful color.

Years ago I found some adorable birthday hats in a shop in Colorado. Although I don't have children, these pint-sized cones were so happy and cute, I bought them anyway, figuring that some day I might have the opportunity to create a birthday party for kids.

My fantasy came true! Decorated with felt flowers, these whimsical hats became the inspiration for the tablecloth, throw pillows, and the overall color palette for a children's birthday party. I often use felt as a decorative fabric because it is affordable, easy to work with, and comes in a great array of colors. I cut paper templates of flowers and dots of different sizes and then traced the shapes directly onto the felt, mixing up all of the bright hues. I made large throw pillows and then glued the felt flowers and some shiny sequins directly onto them. I used the same process to create the tablecloth, where the added polka dots and flowers gave it a lively texture.

I bought multicolored candy lollipops and swirled suckers in the same shades as the felt to create candy "bouquets." I filled glass vases with colorful bubblegum balls to hold the lollipops in place and trimmed the containers with multicolored ribbon and miniature felt flowers.

For refreshments, I served all the goodies I loved as a child: popcorn, cotton candy, chocolate cupcakes with gobs of white icing and sprinkles, Heart-shaped Grilled Cheese Sandwiches (page 235), red, blue, and green Kool-Aid, and homemade ice cream. Candies, bubblegum balls, and giant jawbreakers completed the table adornments. Although there were a few sugar rushes later, after everyone got home, at the time, party guests all had a blast (adults included!).

Create a theme and stick to it. Clockwise from top left: Every detail of the party is complementary, from the drinks with bright straws and little parasols to the cones, decorated with sequins and ribbons, that hold popcorn. Clear plates allow the jazzy felt flowers to show through. Using wrapping paper from my collection, I crafted more hats (below right and center, and left) as well the cotton candy sticks (right). The computer has given us the capability to make wonderful affordable invitations. I printed a bright stripe to play off the party theme, embellishing the front with mini felt flowers and sequins. A cute insert provides the pertinent details. Even the cupcakes decorated with sprinkles and candies are a design element. Lollipop "bouquets" have goodies for the munchkins to eat or take home.

From preparation to party time: Children get a kick out of dressing up, and these whimsical hats provided that element of fun.

summer

The heat of the summer should not dissuade us from entertaining. All of the season's wonders—the tastes, textures, and sights—of the beach at sunset, the roadside stands and local farmers' markets filled with flowers and an abundant harvest of fresh produce, and the sound of the waves rolling in—all of summer's images are intoxicating enough to delight and energize us to throw a party. After all, the warm weather months provide a gift to the senses—so why not indulge?

For me, summer is a big time of year for birthdays—and I celebrate a number of them on the following pages, from a party I gave for my mother and aunt, to a sunflower soiree held in honor of my Leo pals, to the ultimate birthday bash to celebrate America's Independence Day in patriotic red, white, and blue. Everybody loves celebrating the Fourth of July!

During the months of June, July, and August, I like to entertain outdoors, favoring green lawns, flowering gardens, the reflection of beautiful decorations in a pond or pool, and the lively, casual mood invoked when guests congregate informally before lunch or dinner. The ultimate alfresco moment, of course, is a picnic, which can be inspired by many things—mine was prompted by a red lacquer umbrella I had brought home from Paris. Armed with a moveable feast and the cool shade the umbrella provided in an unexpected location at Weatherstone, I surprised guests with an afternoon that was stylish, relaxing, and truly memorable.

birthday bash for the Beaty girls

ON A SUMMER AFTERNOON, THE FAMILY
GATHERS TO REMEMBER GOLDEN DAYS AND
CREATE MEMORIES AT A LANDMARK CELEBRATION.

Preceding pages: Set among the trees, a table brimming with dozens of daisies invites guests to be seated.
This page: Cousins and friends take a moment to share a memory book filled with photos. Opposite page: Color and geometry come into focus with wide blue and white stripes that play off the graphic simplicity of the flowers.

A collection of blue and white porcelain is placed around

the pool, echoing the crisp stripes on the long tables.

This page: At dusk, candles glow on the birthday cake while guests take snapshots, children play with sparklers, and Mom and my aunt get ready to make a wish.
Opposite page: Sugary hydrangeas, daisies, and a butterfly embellish a white cake created by Sylvia Weinstock.

This page: A cool, shady area where guests can sit is essential for a summer soiree. Porcelain barrels serve as a place to set drinks or a small plate of hors d'oeuvres. Opposite page: Lounge chairs line up outside the trellised space.

What better excuse is there to bring people together on a warm summer day than to celebrate a birthday? On this July evening, we were actually celebrating two—my mom's seventy-fifth in August, and my Aunt June's eightieth in June. Guests came to Weatherstone from all over the country to join the fun and honor the Beaty girls.

Mom and I share a love of blue and white, so naturally that was the color scheme I chose for the party. On the long outdoor tables was a big, bold, cornflower-blue striped fabric that I'd lugged back from Paris a few years back and stored until I'd found the perfect use for it. Bunches of daisies always look fresh, and their button center and white petals create a counterpoint of dots to the stripes, always a pleasing and visually strong effect. At outdoor parties, I try to keep the look chic but low-key by mixing elements—I used inexpensive blue glasses, blue hurricane lamps, white tin plates, and reproduction willowware china (plus some pieces of the real thing). Blue and white porcelain planters and garden seats were placed around the pool, and pillows in a pretty tile print tied into the overall scheme. As guests relaxed before supper, they looked through a memory book I'd made of the two sisters, starting back to when they were little girls and highlighting elements of their lives.

For dinner, guests could choose between lobster as the main course, prepared in the simplest manner possible—a special touch for my aunt, who's from the Midwest and likes to have it in the summertime when she comes east—or Marinated Flank Steak (page 235), both accompanied by Farro Salad (page 236). I also catered to the other relatives who came to the party with gifts of photos of loved ones, placed in silver picture frames and wrapped in paper I'd made by scanning in a tile pattern. I used the tile's center motif for both gift wrap and cards. As the sun set, sparklers lit up the night, wishes were made, and the Beaty sisters raised a toast to another beautiful year.

155 Years of the Beaty Girls

Steamed Lobster with Herbed Lemon Butter
Marinated Sliced Flank Steak

Farro Salad with Vegetable and Mint
Garden Greens Vinaigrette
Corn on the Cob

Birthday Cake
Homemade Ice Cream

Champagne

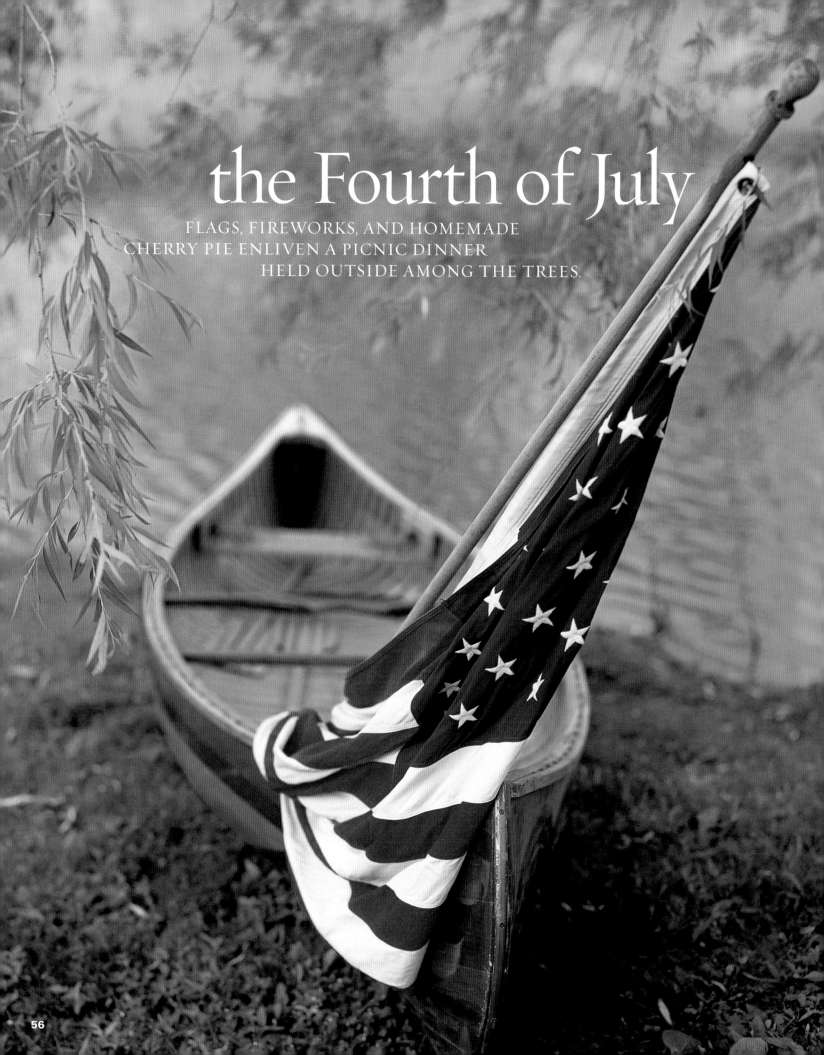

the Fourth of July

FLAGS, FIREWORKS, AND HOMEMADE
CHERRY PIE ENLIVEN A PICNIC DINNER
HELD OUTSIDE AMONG THE TREES.

This page: Pillar candles are set inside hurricane lamps placed next to a row of miniature flags stuck in white pots. Opposite page: Old Glory shows off her colors.

By situating the tables between the ponds, guests see a pretty reflection of the colors and decorations in the water. A seating area nearby provides another place for friends and family to gather to talk.

A row of American flags sets the stage for a colorful repetition of patriotic hues, from striped napkins to lanterns in alternating colors.

R

ed, white, and blue makes a graphic

statement on a picnic table for an outdoor get-together.

 party for the Fourth of July invites certain expectations—that guests will celebrate outside on a hot summer day, that food will be all-American fare, and that the festivities will end with a bang—literally—in a display of fireworks. I like parties with expectations, because it's fun to welcome guests to a classic celebration, while surprising them with unexpected touches.

I enjoy entertaining under the trees at Weatherstone, my home in Sharon, Connecticut, and for this event, I found a pretty spot situated between two ponds, so the colors of the decorations were reflected in the water. Using painted red poles secured in buckets and swathes of georgette for a canopy, I set up an eating area using picnic tables with planks painted red, white, and blue (no need for linens!). Paper lanterns in patriotic colors floated above the tables, providing the exclamation point to all the stripes.

For the main meal, I kept it simple: Barbecued Baby Back Ribs with Rhubarb Barbecue Sauce (page 236) and grilled chicken were served with Zesty Baked Beans (page 237), cole slaw, deviled eggs, and tomato and Vidalia onion salad on white tin plates. Stars were everywhere: I painted red and white trays, using cut-to-measure plywood and molding; a local bakery created mini blue patriot cakes that I topped with white stars cut from marzipan; a Sour Cherry Pie (page 237) had a similar design.

While the event went without a hitch, I remember one year when a huge thunderstorm promised to turn the party into a soggy mess. Luckily, I was able to put everything on the porch, and by the time guests were ready for the display of sparklers, the weather had cleared and expectations were fulfilled.

Carolyne Roehm

Invitation

American Celebration

July 4, 2004

Weatherstone

Sharon, CT

July 4 2004

July 4 2004

Barbecued Ribs

Grilled Chicken

Baked Beans

Deviled Eggs

Cole Slaw

Tomato & Vidalia Salad

Sour Cherry Pie

Patriot Cakes

Vanilla Ice cream

S heer georgette panels create the sense of a

Brightly painted poles hold up filmy canopies of georgette in colors of the American flag. Small paper globes are hung at varying heights above the table.

festive outdoor party room that is pretty, breezy, and open.

For me, a lot of the fun of entertaining is setting up the
decorations. **This page:** Have all of your party "props"
on hand along with the tableware. I put the elements in
big straw carryalls to make them easy to transport.
Opposite page: The planks of the picnic table are painted,
so there's no need for a tablecloth.

O nce the party is in full swing, I love to

Scenes from the party. **Opposite page:** Even Ruffie gets into the spirit of things with a stars-and-stripes kerchief. **This page:** As the sun goes down, candles are lit on the table while guests chat at dinner.

look around at all my guests and see the happy faces.

The grand finale: At night, a sparkling display

was set up right in the middle of an allee of trees.

Sunflowers add a seasonal jolt of color, accenting the black and white stripes of the tabletop decor. When planning a party, I like to think seasonally for both decorations and food—the look and mood will be more cohesive and economical.

sunflower soirée

BOLD STRIPES AND BRILLIANT
BLOOMS ENERGIZE AN AUGUST DINNER
DANCE AT A BEAUTIFUL BEACH HOUSE.

An ideal setting: The strong lines of the tented cabana work well with the chic black and white motif. Better than any other blooms, sunflowers, with their leonine manes of petals, seem fitting at a party for Leos—the astrological kings of the jungle.

*A*lways use lots of candles on your

table. We all like to look glamorous, so no overhead lighting!

Sunflowers are one of summer's gifts to us, and at this birthday celebration held in August for several Leo friends, this cheerful flower became a bold design motif. Gayfyrd Steinberg offered her great beach house for this event, and her pool cabana begged for graphic black and white stripes, with the sunflowers as huge punctuation points. We found a source for the sunflowers right out on Long Island, and this gave us ample ammunition to make a bold statement with huge bouquets of sunflowers in oversized black pots. The flower itself is full of a sunny energy that is so pleasing to the eye you can use it again and again without diminishing its visual impact. Now that sunflowers are readily available during the late summer and early fall at grocery stores and florists, it is easy to buy an armful if you don't grow them yourself.

I started with a plain white invitation, then on the computer added a dark border and a sunflower at the top above a pretty script. (I used a similar design for the menu cards on the table.) Bright yellow envelopes were lined in black and white striped paper and tied with a matching ribbon.

Stripes and polka dots are two of my favorite designs, and I made use of both for this summer party. Tables were covered in black and white striped fabric and set with beautiful white china and bowls of bright sunflowers. With their velvety button centers and colorful fringe of petals, the blooms punctuated the linear look of the table in a vibrant way. The tiered bar stacked with glasses also played off the linear stripes, and was flanked with silver bowls filled with limes and lemons, which served as a pretty note of color. The menu featured Jambalaya (page 238).

The theme was reiterated on the birthday cakes made by my friend Sylvia Weinstock, who replicated the sunflowers and stripes on individual cakes. (They looked almost too good to eat!) Even the presents picked up the graphic mood. To change it up a bit, black-eyed Susans took the place of sunflowers on the black and white striped packages, and I varied the width of the stripes on the wrapping and ribbon to make things even more lively.

Summer is the time for bold, clean graphics and giant sunflowers. Clockwise from top left: A black and white striped table keeps it simple with silver salt and pepper shakers, beautiful white china, and a vase of sunflowers. The tiered bar is practical (you can stack multiples of glassware), but looks visually impressive as well. The invitations had a sunflower motif. Stash limes in shiny silver bowls at the bar. Individual birthday cakes made by Sylvia Weinstock and gifts echo the party motifs. Serve wine in decanters. Striped cushions provide comfortable seating.

e inventive: Stack glasses on a pyramid of

shelves; fill giant clamshells with ice and bottled drinks.

This page: For this party, sunflowers reigned. Notice that the leaves were left on the stems, contributing a touch of green. Opposite page: After painting a carpet of large black and white stripes on the dance floor, I arranged dozens of sunflowers in standing black urns nearby.

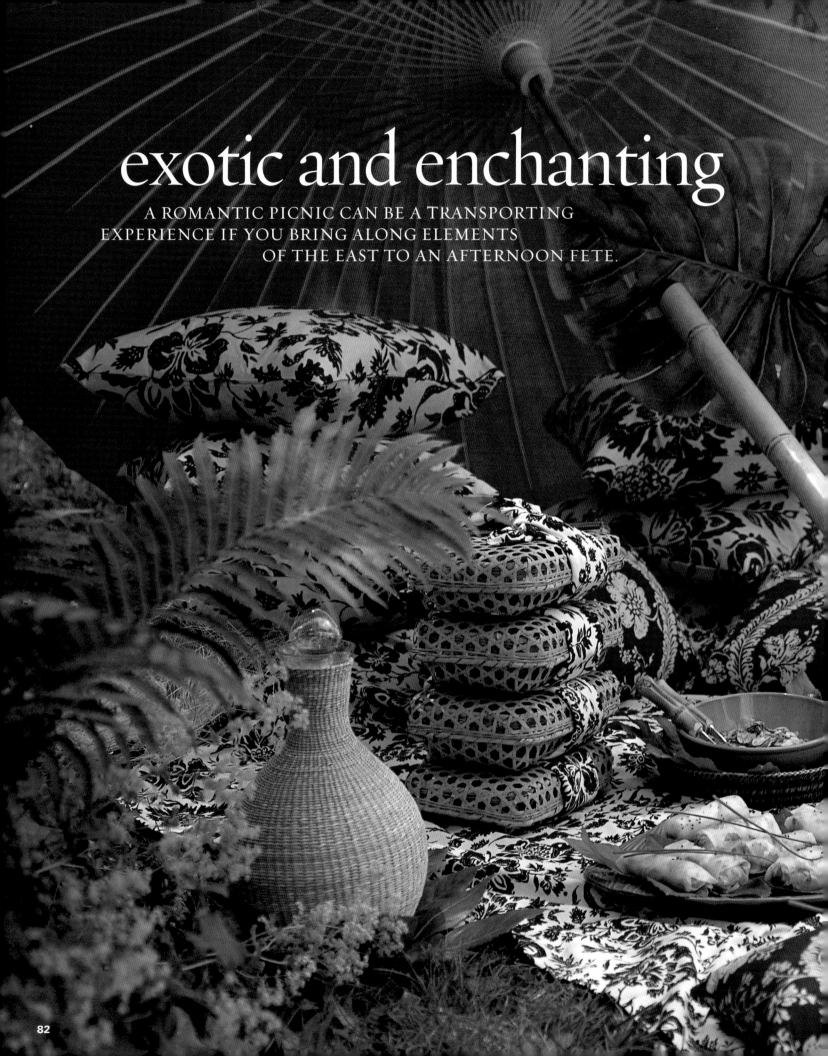

exotic and enchanting

A ROMANTIC PICNIC CAN BE A TRANSPORTING
EXPERIENCE IF YOU BRING ALONG ELEMENTS
OF THE EAST TO AN AFTERNOON FETE.

When planning your picnic, find a secluded location, such as under a willow tree or near a stream. Or if a park is your choice, create your own space with an oversized umbrella—your ingenuity will charm your guests.

This page: The red-lacquered Chinese umbrella has a story behind it: I spotted it in a shop in Paris and it caused quite a stir in the Paris airport as I lugged it through the terminal. Opposite page: I have always liked to mix prints—here Chinese and Indonesian fabrics in red and white are combined for the pillows, tablecloth, and napkins.

Creating a special environment for a party is one of the most exciting things a host or hostess can do for guests. I love that "ahh" moment when the stage is set and the guests first gaze upon the room, the table, and the decorations. I always want to transport my guests, if only for a few hours, away from the everyday and the mundane. The elements of a party do not have to be expensive, overly complex, or grand, but to be memorable I think they have to be original. That's the real challenge for any host or hostess.

When I started dreaming about this Asian-themed picnic, I thought immediately about the red-lacquered umbrella I had found and brought home from Paris. It became the inspiration for this afternoon event. I

settled on a location, set away under a willow tree, and toted a tablecloth for the ground, patterned pillows for seating, and of course, that big Chinese umbrella. Bamboo lunch boxes with chopsticks were tied with napkins; a rattan tray for drinks, bamboo-handled cutlery, and a lined bamboo pitcher of chilled Portuguese Vinho Verde came along as well. My miniature Schnauzer, Sassy, brought up the rear.

When it's hot outside, the menu should be light, but satisfying. I settled on Shrimp Spring Rolls with a spicy Sesame Dipping Sauce (page 239) and Crisp Radish Salad (page 239) for lunch, and easy-to-eat Lemon Curd Tartlets (page 240) to finish off the afternoon meal.

Left to right: Leaf- and fish-shaped bowls hold a spicy sesame sauce, black sesame seeds, and crunchy Chinese noodles. I used the bamboo baskets for lunch boxes, but you could use them to hold party favors as well. I grow radishes in my garden; when thinly sliced and tossed with a rice vinegar vinaigrette, they make an attractive counterpart to the shrimp rolls.

autumn

We give thanks for autumn's abundance in many ways. How can we resist celebrating the vivid colors and magnificent harvest of bittersweet, squash, pumpkins, apples, and pears that greet us in the fall months? The trees show off their gorgeous hues, decorating the landscape in ways that delight the senses and set the stage for entertaining in bigger-than-life ways.

I enjoy hosting enormous parties during this time of year, including the barn dance at Weatherstone with its spirited square-dancing and indulgent desserts, or the annual Hunt Ball, where the gentlemen wear classic hunting pinks and women dress up in satin gowns. For me, giving a party allows me to indulge in a fantasy, creating a special moment in time where guests can shake off their everyday worlds and participate in a new one. The parties on the following pages document those unbridled moments, capturing images that I hope will inspire and help you to create your own.

Halloween is a particularly special fantasy for me. I suppose it brings out the child in everyone, but these days, it's often a holiday that engenders the most predictable party décor and treats. The one I dreamed up injects a little magic and spookiness back into it. And looking at the photographs, I think I can safely say I accomplished what I set out to do. Even I'm a bit surprised by the ghostliness of the cobwebbed tableau, silvery jack o' lanterns, and skeletal guests in attendance!

autumn barn dance

A LOVE OF DANCING AND FALL'S VIVID
HUES SPARK A HARVEST DINNER
AND A NIGHT OF DOWN-HOME FUN.

In the fall, I always feel invigorated when nature begins its transformation into a landscape of astounding color. The beauty of it is something I like to share, and years ago I started inviting guests for an autumn dance and harvest dinner. I grew up in the Midwest, where children were taught to square dance in school, and I have found that nothing breaks the ice and frees up inhibitions like kicking up one's heels with a few do-si-dos.

My guide for the decoration and the food for the party was Mother Nature—from the vibrant hues of the much-celebrated sugar maples to the homey smells of the first fires of the season. All the vegetation for the decor was gathered at Weatherstone, on country roads, and from the local farmers. Apples from the orchard and sprays of rose hips were heaped on tables under a centerpiece of still-leafy branches. I found reproduction paisley shawls for tablecloths, which I placed on burlap underskirts. Brass candlesticks glimmered with candles in burnt umber, orange, sienna, and deep red. Behind the table set for seventy guests, David Monn created glowing magic with giant corn stacks and the ultimate harvest moon. Fallen leaves were collected and piled around the dance floor. (They looked great, but the cleanup the next day was quite a chore!) Bales of hay topped with oversized linen pillows made fun sofas for weary dancers to collapse upon between reels, and an empty hay wagon served as the bandstand for two guitarists, two fiddlers, and the callers for the dance.

This rustic ambience required the appropriate fare, and in the kitchen, my staff, including Nancy Quantrini and Margarida de Carvalho, outdid themselves. Spanish terra-cotta casseroles were filled with Smothered Chicken in a rich curry-laced gravy (page 240) and ribs that had been baked until the meat was falling off the bone. Garlic and Rosemary Potatoes (page 241), a medley of autumn squashes, and jalapeño pepper corn bread served with red pepper jelly were polished off with a frisee salad tossed with pecans and Stilton. We felt no guilt treating ourselves to the desserts—Bread Pudding with Bourbon Sauce (page 241) and Pumpkin Pie (page 242—as we knew we would be able to dance off the indulgences. Well fed, we all rolled onto the dance floor and swung the night (and some of the calories) away!

Nature provided many of the decorations I used for
the celebration. Apples and autumn leaves adorn a
paisley-topped table in the room where we had
cocktails. On the dinner table are two sources of light—
tall candles in fall colors and small white votives.

eautiful lighting is paramount at every

This page: Square dancing brings out the best in everyone. It's a fun way for guests who don't know each other to interact. **Opposite page:** Spanish casseroles filled with Smothered Chicken and St. Louis spareribs are served family style, alongside seasonal vegetables. Spanish wine carafes hold red and white wine, beer, and apple cider.

successful party—a mix of sources creates a radiant effect.

I chose the colors for the dance floor from the table-cloth that dressed the sixty-foot dining table. An overhead trellis of poles serves as the anchor for large paper lanterns and branches of autumn leaves. Following pages: Snapshots capture the day of preparation. David Monn devised a Monster Moon ten feet in diameter.

a Dickens-inspired Halloween

JOIN THE GHOSTS (ALONG WITH
SPIDERWEBS, SKELETONS, AND SUGARPLUM
FAIRIES) TO CREATE A LITTLE MISCHIEF
AT A MEMORABLE PARTY FOR KIDS.

Silver, gray, and black take the place of traditional Halloween orange. This page: I spray-painted eighty-eight jack o' lanterns gleaming silver and used them as the central decoration. Opposite page: A super-sized ghost was hoisted outside the window, and as night fell, dry ice created a ghostly "fog" around it.

I have always loved Halloween. I suppose it is natural for a fashion designer to gravitate to this holiday, given all the opportunities it presents to let the imagination fly. My love of costume design was seeded in those first Halloween costumes I made as a little girl. When my French goddaughter and her mother proposed a trip to the United States near the end of October, I thought, "Aha!" Here was an opportunity to show them a fun, quintessentially American tradition.

Instead of making this a black and orange color scheme, I worked with a palette of silver, gray, and black and wanted my party table to resemble Miss Havisham's decaying banquet room in Charles Dickens's *Great Expectations.* Cobwebs, fog, and a look of disheveled splendor became the theme.

The party was held in my studio, a simple, clean space with high ceilings that is an ideal place to create another world. The pair of chandeliers that light it was my starting point: I stretched what seemed like miles of artificial cobwebs from the chandeliers to every corner, then enhanced the gauzy ethereal look by adding bits of dried Spanish moss. I dyed mounds of cheesecloth in varying shades of gray to cover the dinner and buffet tables and create oversized ghosts that hung on the porch and throughout the room. The heads were draped with the gauzy cheesecloth and adorned with sad faces cut from black felt.

Anchored at each end of the dining table were barren artificial trees draped in faux spiderwebs and moss and filled with faux bats, black crows, and a large stuffed owl. Dilapidated candelabra with black candles, rubber snakes, spiders, and silver pumpkins made up the tableau. Sinister hosts—creepy skeletons rented from New York City's Abracadabra costume shop presided and were so realistic they were truly frightening to some. Each child had his or her fortune told by "Madame Rosa" (who works with me). With some advance help from a mom or dad, she was able to impress the children with her insider knowledge of their hobbies, school life, and friendships.

For food, we had genuine kids' fare, but the adults seemed to love the food every bit as much! On the menu were homemade Sesame Chicken Fingers with Peach Honey Sauce (page 243), Cookie-Cutter French Fries (page 243), macaroni and cheese, baby hamburgers and hot dogs, salad, and treats— homemade popcorn balls, ice cream, and individual black widow spider cakes mounted on caramelized sugar webs. Guests received the obligatory trick-or-treat candy to take home. No one refused the goody bag!

Not every costume has to be ghoulish. Four little friends are a quintet of sugarplum fairies decked out in flowers and pastel tulle. I made masks and headdresses out of flowers that matched ballerina skirts, dyed turtlenecks, and cotton tights in lavender, pink, ice blue, and soft mint.

For the party, my studio became a maze of cobwebs, moss, and fog, created from discreetly hidden buckets of dry ice. As it began to get dark, the fog swirled around the room (with the help of a fan) as eerie sounds greeted the tricksters. Out of the mists, two friends—one as an oversized ghost and the other an enormous black crow—chased and taunted the children into giggles.

Ask adults to join in the fun. **This page:** I dressed up as a witch, swathed in black tulle, and organized the fun and games. **Opposite page:** A friend, disguised as a giant specter, managed to scare the children into believing he was real.

Eerie means mysterious, strange, and unexpected

—very much like the way pastels seem on All Hallows' Eve.

S pooky details delight guests, who are treated to

This page: Cobwebbed candlesticks put the "boo" in a beautiful table. This page: My godchild Volga as a blue fairy is unfazed by her creepy skeletal dinner partner. Opposite page: The evil witch chases the good sugarplum fairies into the party.

dinner at a table Miss Havisham would have loved.

A scary affair. **This page:** Each guest's place was marked by a glow-in-the-dark skeleton's head (left). Overseen by a giant ghostly server, the buffet table stands ready for the food (right). **Opposite page:** Sylvia Weinstock's black widow spider cakes were a huge success. Following pages: Snapshots capture the highlights, from preparation to party time.

the hunt ball

CRISP AUTUMN AIR AND A GLORIOUS
MORNING RIDING TO THE HOUNDS SET
THE MOOD FOR THE NIGHT'S FESTIVITIES.

The centuries-old tradition of hunting has changed very little over time, especially in the care and breeding of both the horses and the hounds, although there is a more benevolent attitude toward the foxes.

I live in horse country, and the social highlight of the fall season is the Millbrook Hunt Ball. The hunting is rather benign—no foxes are killed—but when it comes to partying, the members of the hunt love to kick up their heels. Last year, the chairs of the event asked if I would consider holding it in my stable in Connecticut and handling the decorating as well. I think I said yes merely because I love how elegant the gentlemen look in their hunting pinks and white tie!

Hunting is based upon tradition and ceremony, and it became instantly clear to me that the decorations would be inspired by the signature green of the hunt that is in the Millbrook Hunt Ball logo, as well as the colors of the season (autumn russet) and of the formal attire worn by the masters of the hunt (their scarlet "pinks"). Two of those hues—green and russet—are found in beautiful magnolia leaves; they became the "flowers" for the party. Masses of magnolia branches were transformed into enormous topiaries

and large bouquets, and were also used as part of the centerpieces, set in bronze urns. To brighten the room and the tables, I brought in brass candlesticks and surrounded each bouquet of magnolias with cattails I had cut from my ponds, and fruits and squashes I had sprayed gold. The shiny fruits glimmered beautifully amid the candlelight on the bronze-colored tablecloths.

I designed the dance floor as a brown and green checkerboard bordered in hunt red and painted a matching hunt emblem logo using a stencil I made. The same logo detailed the evening's program and the take-home remembrance.

For the ball committee, I hosted a cocktail party for 150 at the house, and Nancy Quantrini, my cook, prepared the canapés. Fortunately, a member of the hunt is Michele Jean, who owns several restaurants, and he and his staff prepared a delicious dinner for the 375 guests!

Old and young guests love being out in nature and watching the tradition of hunting, which requires skill, patience, and sportsmanship.

I t is a thrill to dress to the nines occasionally,

This page: The beauty of the formal hunt attire, the elegance of the ladies in long gowns, and the sophistication of gentlemen in white tie reminds me of another era that is much more glamorous than the one we live in today. **Opposite page:** Dusk at Weatherstone.

especially for a traditional event like the Hunt Ball.

Guests gather in small groups to share stories and sip Champagne at a cocktail party for members of the Hunt Ball committee.

The candles and fireplaces are blazing, canapés are being passed to the sound of clinking Champagne glasses, and the sound of laughter is heard throughout the rooms— all combine to create a magical aura.

This page: At the cocktail party, canapés included Gravlax with Crème Fraîche and Mustard (page 244) and Prosciutto-wrapped Cherry Tomatoes in Parmesan Cups (page 244). **Opposite page:** The traditional scarlet coats, or "pinks," are worn only by the masters of the hunt.

I love the feeling of anticipation as we wait for

When the house is aglow and music fills the air,
I relax and enjoy the magical atmosphere that is
the end result of all the planning and preparation.
My own little pack of "hounds" does too!

all of the party guests to arrive. Dogs included!

A change of place or venue during a party creates mystery and excitement. After cocktails at the house, the guests proceed up the hill to the barn for dinner and dancing.

This page: Three hundred and seventy-five people dined and danced, truly to the wee hours of the morning. The last diehards left at 3:00 AM! Opposite page: Each season provides the materials for eye-catching decorations. Here cattails mixed with magnolia leaves create a striking centerpiece with gold spray-painted baby pumpkins, pears, grapes, and gourds.

Opposite: It took four days to paint the dance floor and walkway into a large-scale checkerboard with the hunt emblem in the center. The barn was tented in hunt-red chiffon, which draped down behind the oversized magnolia topiaries (like the one shown here) and the bandstand. Following pages: Close-ups of preparations and the end result—the checkerboard and logo show up on the programs and the gift bags for the guests.

holiday entertaining

There are many things I love about the Christmas season (and a few I do not!). I still get excited about the first snowfall, and when I awaken to a snowy Christmas morning in New England or Aspen or even New York City, for that matter, I am always in awe of how beautiful nature is.

The scents of Christmas give warmth and life to a home and evoke fond memories—balsam, evergreens, baking cookies and cakes, mulled cider, spiced wine, the nutmeg in eggnog, forced paperwhite blossoms and pine cones in a crackling fire. I love the sounds of Christmas, too, from popular songs such as Irving Berlin's "White Christmas" and the traditional tunes of carolers, to sleigh bells and church bells and beautiful religious music.

But more than anything, it's the preparation for Christmas that gives me a thrill. I feel a real joy in creating and wrapping presents, finding the tree, decorating the house, and planning dinners and parties.

Through the years, I have hosted a variety of Christmas get-togethers, including caroling parties, ice-skating afternoons, casual big buffets, formal dinners, black-tie dances, and small musical evenings. The holidays allow us to think beyond the normal dinner party and devise special moments, providing us all, both hosts and guests, with the best of memories.

During the holidays, making time to be with the people you love is what the season is all about. No matter what size or style your party—big, small, simple, or formal—allow yourself to catch up with your guests. In other words, enjoy the moment you have created!

'tis the season

PREPARING THE HOUSE FOR THE HOLIDAY
SEASON IS HALF THE FUN OF CHRISTMAS.

Finding a tree tall enough for my twenty-four-foot ceilings is always a challenge. Throughout the years, I have collected an array of multicolored decorations for the tree, but the rest of the house is trimmed in tranquil green and white. I use white quince, paperwhites, white roses, tulips, and carnations as my principal flowers at Christmas; wreaths and garlands are a mix of evergreens tied with moss-colored ribbon.

Some years, I decorate more than others, depending on my mood and how much entertaining I plan for the season. When I am in full decorating mode, all of the windows in the house sport wreaths, and the three flights of stairs and gallery balusters are draped in garlands.

Creating beautiful presents is always a joy, and every year, I concoct a different gift-wrapping scheme. At times, my packages are truly elaborate, but I also like the very simple ones shown here, where I mixed multi-colored miniature Christmas balls with bright satin ribbons and foil papers.

njoy the spirit of the season, where everyone

I have a terrific household staff that helps me do everything. After decorating, I like to treat everyone with a light supper of Mini Lemon Crêpes Stuffed with Lobster (page 245). My beloved puppy, Lucky, is always nearby to give me support while the other seven dogs are off playing or sleeping!

comes together (even pups!) to help with the decorating.

I had not given a cocktail party in years. I normally prefer to have dinners, where one can sit and have a conversation. But one of the advantages of this kind of get-together is that preparation is relatively simple, from arranging for the drinks and hors d'oeuvres such as Mini BLTs (page 245) to hiring a good pianist for entertainment.

Christmastime in the city

151

A NEW APARTMENT IN NEW YORK CALLED FOR A
COCKTAIL PARTY AND IMPROMPTU HOUSEWARMING.

During the busy holiday season, a cocktail party allows one to see many friends at once. Although there's nothing formal about such a gathering, people still like to dress up a bit and enjoy stopping by to have a chat, a drink, and a bite to eat.

There are many ways of entertaining, but once in a while an old-fashioned "drinks party" is fun. It allows us to connect briefly and wish many friends good health and prosperity. Thanks to a terrific pianist, a number of my guests stayed later and sang a carol or two!

It is important to make things memorable for children, so I created a candy cane–inspired table for my young coworkers. I used red and white felt for the tablecloth and decorated it with matching ornaments and with candles that were lit as daylight faded. This last special touch gave the kids a feeling of having a "grown-up" experience.

a holiday tradition

MAKE A SIMPLE TRADITION OF BAKING
HOLIDAY COOKIES INTO A
MEMORABLE EVENT
FOR BOTH YOUNG
AND OLD.

Having fun and sharing the experience of baking is undoubtedly more important and more memorable than creating the perfect "designer" cookies. Still, it was nice to showcase our efforts in something special, so I provided tissue paper and dotted ribbon to present the finished work (opposite page).

Opposite page: The breakfast room at Weatherstone is filled with light and made a great place for both the work and the party.
This page: My helpers loved their very own cookie-decorating aprons that I made out of felt to match the tablecloths.

My family has always had a tradition of decorating cookies at Christmastime. Call us old-fashioned, but we stick to simple Spiced Sugar Cookies with Royal Icing (page 246) instead of going for a flashy mix of sweets. But what we lack in variety, we make up for with all kinds of decorating sugars and icings—I love the results! The art of today's cookie making goes far beyond what we did back in the fifties and sixties, but those winter days spent with my mother and aunt are still a source of fond memories. As an adult, I have continued that tradition with friends and their children. This year, after enlisting the help of some young pals, I decided to make an event of it by serving lunch as well (a little homemade vegetable soup helps to counterbalance the sugar intake from all of the "testing" we had to do on the cookies and icing). I believe in teaching children the importance of traditions and how simple things like decorating cookies can be creative and fun. It is a nice way to get them away from the TV and computer games.

To make the cookie work a bit easier, I limited the color palette to red, green, and white, and used only four cookie-cutter shapes. (I have a giant box of cutters, but decided to remain focused on just a few.) I provided tins, so that after all the baking was done, each participant was able to take home a red and white gift tin of his or her creations.

You are Invited

To a

Cookie decorating party

On December 17 2006

At 2:00 pm

22 Herrick Road

Sharon, CT 06069

From top left: Traditional Christmas crackers, which I filled with goodies, were at each place setting at the lunch. After the cookies were finished, we put them in white tins and decorated them with tissue, tags, and ribbons from my Christmas gift-wrapping collection. Details are important in creating a memorable event; these little stockings filled with sweets were attached to each mug of homemade soup. I love the play of geometric patterns in different-sized dots and stripes. I asked teenage friends Susanna and Hope to help the younger kids with the decorating. A special little friend, Aidan, stopped by in his Santa suit.

Christmas eve at Weatherpebble

VIBRANT ILEX BERRIES INSPIRE THE DECOR FOR A
FAMILY GET-TOGETHER, WHERE GUESTS SIT DOWN
TO A BEAUTIFUL RED TABLE, REPLETE WITH GIFTS.

This page: At the center of the room, a roaring fire and glowing red candles call attention to a portrait framed in ilex berries. Floral jacquard shawls from India are draped over the couch and used on the table to create a warm ambiance. Opposite page: Everyone dresses comfortably for the cozy night.

We jokingly refer to my mother's house as the Little House or Weatherpebble. When the big house, Weatherstone, burned down in 1999, I moved into Weatherpebble for three years as I rebuilt. I was fortunate to have the option of this space, which was once a carriage house, but had been redone years ago into a guest house with a large, wood-paneled central room and a lovely fireplace. This welcoming room became a haven after the fire and the scene of many a happy evening.

It is a great space for a family dinner at Christmastime. The wood paneling looks amazing when dressed up with any color, but it stands out particularly well with red. On a recent trip to India, I had purchased some exquisite red damask shawls, which I used throughout the room.

To create my red-on-red theme, I bought a large quantity of fabulous ilex berries to create a centerpiece and decorate the fireplace mantel and other unexpected spots. The Christmas tree was adorned with only red ornaments.

Because the ilex was so luscious, I wanted to do a very large bouquet in the middle of the table. I placed four tall nineteenth-century candlesticks with red candles around the ilex, which created a beautiful rosy glow, illuminating the red glass and tableware, red napkins, and damask tablecloth. Each guest had a small gift at his or her place that was wrapped to coordinate with all of the ruby hues in the room.

A delicious dinner of my favorite holiday fare—including cream of chestnut soup with a dollop of cumin cream, Glazed Veal Chops (page 247), Puree of Squash with Fried Sage Butter (page 247), Braised Endive (page 247), and a mixed vegetable medley—was followed by a parfait glacée Grand Marnier and homemade shortbread. We sat down to dinner on the early side to ensure we were all in bed early enough for Santa to arrive.

This page: A large centerpiece can present sight-line difficulties at a dinner party. With longer branches, one can keep all of the volume at the top and cluster very short branches at the base, allowing the guests to see through the midsection of the arrangement. **Following pages:** A glowing fire, gifts galore in red embossed papers, and a satisfying dinner work together to create a magical night.

Christmas in Aspen

SLOW DOWN THE PACE AT HOLIDAY TIME
BY ENTERTAINING IN WAYS THAT
ARE RELAXED AND SIMPLE, YET STYLISH.

Joy to the world. This page: For my first Christmas in Aspen, I created decorations using all natural elements. Opposite page: Evergreens, mulberry leaves, and red berry branches in silver vases look fresh and festive on nineteenth-century horn furniture; paintings get a similar embellishment.

Inspired by my memories of European chalets decorated with alpine motifs, for my Christmas Eve dinner I used stag antler candlesticks and flatware, emerald stemware, and deer-motif porcelain from Austria on a velveteen tablecloth. A small gift tied with green satin ribbon awaits each guest.

Normally, I spend the holidays at Weatherstone, which always involves huge amounts of decorating and entertaining. I love that time of the year with its endless holiday fun. But in my second winter season in Aspen, I decided to celebrate Christmas in Colorado, where I knew it would be quiet and simple.

Perched on the Roaring Fork River, my place has an unobstructed view of Independence Pass, so you have a strong sense of the great outdoors. I decorated the house in fresh evergreens and pinecones and adorned antique mounted antlers, big mirrors, and oil paintings with coronets of evergreens tied on with moss-colored velvet ribbon. White lights and pinecone ball ornaments were all that was needed on the tree, and the flickering candles and glowing embers in the two wood-burning fireplaces provided the only glitter in the rooms. Fresh cherries, a pretty bowl of fruit, and brightly wrapped presents contributed notes of color.

The Christmas Eve menu was special in many ways, but by no means grand, as I wanted to keep the evening somewhat relaxed. Still, on such a night, dishes should be out of the ordinary, which is why I chose a seafood bisque, Cornish Game Hens (page 248), a timbale of broccoli, Wild Mushroom Risotto Cake (page 248), and an endive and Stilton cheese salad, all topped off with a nice bottle of Château Beychevelle. Dessert was Poached Pears Wrapped in Pastry (page 249), individually served on gold-beaded glass plates; a fruit-nut cake dusted with confectioners' sugar was an enticing alternative.

Although I went back to celebrating Christmas in Connecticut the following year, with a house full of dogs, a cat, and family and friends, I treasure my holiday festivities in Aspen for inspiring creative ways to entertain while enjoying some much-needed moments of tranquility and peace. After all, isn't that what the holidays are supposed to be about?

Play up colors other than traditional holiday hues.
This page: Light the candles and dress a silver bowl of fruit in fresh evergreens.
Following pages: Close-ups reveal the delicious dishes, plus some of the details that tie the theme of the night together, including a gift tag and china embellished with a deer motif, and antler candelabra.

Let the decoration of the holiday gifts reflect the style of your home. To echo the red accents in the decor of my Aspen place, I use red as a prominent color in my Christmas decorations and on the gifts placed around the rooms and under the tree.

uring the holidays, look for ways to use

beautifully wrapped gifts as decorative elements in a room.

winter

One of my favorite books is *Happy Days* by Brendan Gill, published in the seventies. It's been out of print for some time, but I've found it a source of inspiration whenever I am planning a party. The black-and-white photographs capture the romance of an era when dinner parties were perfectly done and the social season was filled with incredible events. While the world has changed in many ways since then, what I love is seeing how those parties fulfilled a longing for magic and a desire to suspend the world for a moment to indulge. I believe that even now you can create that feeling of fantasy on any scale, big or small, when you entertain—you only need inspiration and the energy and desire to do so.

A theme is important when creating a party—it creates, sustains, and brings together your inspiration and fantasy. Your theme can be as simple as a color—white was the impetus behind my New Year's Eve fete—or an annual holiday, the way Valentine's Day was the raison d'etre for an impromptu dinner party for two in Paris. When I stumbled upon a stack of red Chinese lanterns on sale in Chinatown, I snapped up a bunch without knowing when I would use them—but they proved to be a spectacular motif that encouraged me to create a whole party scenario around them. My suggestion to you is simple. When you're planning to entertain, look around: You may find that inspiration is sitting on a table or a shelf right in front of you!

I wanted the decorations to glisten like snow, so the evening's color palette relied on frosted and white surfaces. I placed snow-flecked branches in a white bowl atop a snow-dusted linen tablecloth, using all-white china, crystal, and eighteenth-century silver to complete the simple, elegant tableau. Of course, Champagne was served.

winter
wonderland

WHAT IS PRETTIER THAN FRESHLY
FALLEN SNOW? A TABLE THAT TAKES
ITS CUES FROM A WINTRY LANDSCAPE
FOR AN ELEGANT NEW YEAR'S EVE DINNER.

The tiniest details of the dinner party reinforced the winter wonderland theme.
Opposite page: Iced sugar cookies on a silver tray are a sweet treat at the end of a somewhat formal meal of Almond Soup (page 252); Halibut with Fried Fresh Herbs and Lemon (page 252); a salad of endive, walnuts, slivered pears, and Stilton cheese; and Coconut Flan (page 251).
This page: Instead of holding fresh flowers, these white ceramic vases glisten with a pristine charm all by themselves.

Holiday time is filled with many wonderful sensations. Just the colors of the holidays—the traditional reds and greens of Christmas, icy blues and silvers, burnished gold and pinecone brown—all add up to a visual feast. But in the same way you often desire a simple meal after an incredibly rich banquet, I found that the idea of a winter white dinner party for New Year's Eve seemed very appealing to me. I wanted to keep the dinner small and intimate, even a bit low-key, and the all-white surroundings kept the look of the room elegant.

There's something enchanting about a winter's day right after a blustery storm, when you see everything covered in a blanket of snow. It's the look of that pristine landscape that inspired me to create a winter wonderland indoors at Weatherstone for the dinner. The color palette for the party was easy—pure white and frosted surfaces used for the invitations, decorations, and party favor wrapping, because I wanted everything to glisten like snow. I used a snowflake cookie cutter to trace the invitations on white card stock,

and sent them in a pochette folder filled with snowy glitter instead of a plain envelope. A round table was covered with a snow-dusted linen tablecloth set with all-white china, crystal, and eighteenth-century silver. As a centerpiece, snow-flocked branches were set in a white bowl overflowing with faux snow with slender white taper candles standing nearby. Little white ceramic vases with faux blossoms took the place of bouquets of fresh flowers, and to accent the all-white theme, each guest received a favorite CD placed in a pochette envelope and tied with a silver ribbon. I wrapped additional presents in silver paper, gray velvet ribbon, and a spray of velvet flowers dusted with glitter.

Even the meal took its cues from the color palette. We started with a creamy Almond Soup (page 252), followed by Halibut with Fried Fresh Herbs and Lemon (page 252) and a salad of endive, slivers of pears, walnuts, and Stilton cheese. For dessert, guests could indulge in Coconut Flan (page 251) or nibble on iced sugar cookies. At the stroke of twelve, we toasted the new year with champagne in our pretty winter wonderland.

Take the time to make special invitations that signal the look and mood of your party. **Far left:** Invitations were traced onto white card stock using a snowflake cookie cutter and sent in a pochette folder filled with glitter rather than in a regular envelope. **Above:** To ring in the new year, each guest received a specially chosen CD encased in a pochette and tied with a silver ribbon.

Valentine's Day in Paris

IN THE PINK: PUT AN ELEGANT SPIN
ON A ROMANTIC DINNER WITH ROSES,
CHAMPAGNE, AND LOTS OF SWEETS.

You don't need a roomful of roses for impact. I divided a few bouquets of French garden roses among vases of different heights and set them on a tablecloth with a frothy, candy-colored print.

One February when I was working in Paris, I realized I would not get back to the States in time to share Valentine's Day with my favorite man. In my mind, there are two ways to approach this yearly occasion: Either the woman takes charge and prepares a romantic dinner, or the man kicks into gear and comes up with something beyond the obligatory bouquet of red roses. I have been very lucky, because the men in my life have always gotten into the spirit and created incredibly memorable days and nights for me! But alas, this time I was alone in the most romantic city in the world. I thought, Why not create a dinner for myself?—one that would live up to my fantasies, using all the beauty one can find in this legendary city, from the gorgeous linens and table settings to the fragrant flowers, exquisite candies, and delectable food.

I enlisted the help of two very talented ladies. My photographer and friend Sylvie Becquet provided her apartment to stage the event and her camera to record it. Doris Brenner, who has the best taste in the world,

supplied the lovely tableware and extraordinary linens. I was truly a kid in a candy shop as I created my ultrafeminine table from a glorious selection of goodies. I went to Rungis, the French wholesale market on the outskirts of Paris, and bought the most extraordinary selection of garden roses. I then went to the new Ladurée on the Left Bank for chocolates. While I love their candies and pastries, I'm even more awed by the patisserie's astonishingly beautiful packaging. Understandably, the delectable colors (rose petal, pistachio, and icy mint) inspired my table. I then went off to buy the dinner, which is so easy to do in Paris, with the myriad of specialty food stores. Foie gras, brioche, pink Champagne, a salad, and Crème Brûlée (page 250) created a sublime dinner.

After taking the photographs, Sylvie and I relaxed and toasted our significant others in other parts of the world. We indulged ourselves in the table's visual beauty and enjoyed our feast of elegant French food. Ah, love!

Ladurée's chic packaging (above, right) and the gorgeous hues of French garden roses inspired the colors chosen for the table. Glasses and tableware in soft celadon green and different shades of pink (opposite page) echo the confectionary hues of the candy boxes.

Tall, flowering branches and porcelain Chinese vases make up the centerpiece on a table inspired by Coco Chanel, who loved quilted surfaces, navy and white, and camellias.

bridal shower brunch

TAKE A CLASSIC APPROACH TO A SWEET
CELEBRATION AND TOAST AN UPCOMING
MARRIAGE IN A SOPHISTICATED
COLOR SCHEME OF NAVY AND WHITE.

193

This page: White quilted paper covers party favors tied with navy saddle-stitched ribbon. The sterling silver hearts are charms that could be put on a key ring. Opposite page: Polka dots also made an appearance— as did the classic bridal flower, lily of the valley— on the mini wedding cakes. Ribbons encircle the little treats created by Sylvia Weinstock.

june 14, 2007

C.M.K

The legacy of designer Coco Chanel continues to delight and amaze me, and I often find myself inspired by one of her classic color schemes or signature looks for my parties. She knew, for instance, how appealing navy and white are together, and for this bridal shower, I settled on those two shades for the decorations. A while back, I found this wonderful white quilted paper that reminded me of one of Chanel's signature quilted bags, and I unearthed it from a drawer to wrap up little party favors. I tied them with a navy and white saddle-stitched ribbon (also used to embellish the invitations) that had been printed with the initials of the couple and the date of their wedding. On some of the packages, I used white silk organza camellias (Coco's signature flower). A sterling silver heart was added as a pretty detail and a memento that guests could have engraved and attached to a key ring or charm bracelet.

I started by setting a stage: The tabletop was covered in a leftover fabric from a room I once decorated; the china used was eighteenth-century blue and white Wedgwood. On the napkins was a cipher, which is a monogram where the letters intertwine and turn into a design. That symbol was made into a stamp that was used on the invitations, menu cards, and a little booklet that was like a miniature album for bridesmaids. Other flowers used were carnations, tulips, and ranunculus, all in white and set in vases under a canopy of white cherry blossom branches. Guests enjoyed a tasty Shrimp Risotto (page 251) and toasted the upcoming nuptials with Champagne.

Everything tells a story at a party, so edit out what does not add to the plot. Each of the gifts, all of the printed fabrics, flowers, ribbons, and vases maintain the color scheme and support the overall classic look of the room. Even Coco Chanel's signature white camellia makes an appearance.

raise the red lanterns!

A PARTY ROOM IS TRANSFORMED INTO A
CHINESE PAVILION WITH PAPER GLOBES, FLASHES
OF GOLD, AND SUPER-SIZED FORTUNE COOKIES.

Red and gold hues stand out in this East-West fantasy. Glassware and linens are kept simple, so as not to detract from the touches of gold. Lights are low (white light bulbs were replaced with red ones), and tabletop votives provide tiny, glowing spots.

This page: A colorful canopy of red and black paper lanterns hang from the ceiling of the party room.
Opposite page: Whenever I use paper globes, I vary the height—and sometimes the size—so the lanterns look like they are floating on air.

This page: I added extravagant details such as this Chinese headdress as ornate touches through the room. You don't need a lot of these kinds of embellishments to make an impact. Opposite page: Bright parasols in a variety of sizes and heights peppered the party space.

Of all the reasons for giving a party, the silliest is the one involving the bargain Chinese lanterns. I happened to be in Chinatown doing a favor for someone when I spied red and black paper globes that were half off the regular price. A light went on and I thought, Why not give a Chinese party? I impulsively bought thirty lanterns and took them home. Months later, I came across the lanterns and had a similar epiphany. Why not now? I promptly began to plan and soon realized how many more I needed. The story perfectly fits that old saying, "Going broke from buying bargains."

For the party, I hung the now very expensive lanterns from the ceiling and I decorated the walls with oversized red fans. Cocktails were held at my mother's house, Weatherpebble, and afterwards, we walked to "Carolyne's Chinese Pavilion," where we were greeted with incense and the sounds of Chinese music. Many of the guests got into the spirit and wore Chinese costumes, and to the ladies, I offered red fans and bamboo hats I had sprayed gold. I had hired an authentic Chinese chef, who prepared a menu of new Hong Kong cuisine. (Chicken Satay with Peanut Sauce on page 253 is an easy alternative to the difficult recipes he prepared.) I had also ordered super-sized fortune cookies with our own original sayings inside them. As a party favor, I sprayed small bamboo steamers gold and filled them with home-made sugared pecans (everyone always loves them) for departing guests to keep as a remembrance.

The fun of doing fantasy parties is that one can get in-volved with so many great details. I designed the invitation to set the tone of the event and matched the motifs and script on it to the menus and place cards so there was a cohesive theme. I even dressed the staff in Chinese jackets and hats, which were easy to find in Chinatown.

My studio is built with three sides of French doors, which at night can make the room dark and leave guests staring out into the nighttime void. So I backed the doors and windows with red paper to look like screens and backlit the panels of red from the outside to create a wonderful glow in the room that was very effective with all of the gold centerpieces shimmering off the votives on the tables. I also thought it would be fun to have oversized lazy Susans on the table instead of serving bowls. My staff figured out how to make them and we lacquered the surfaces a bright Chinese red. They looked quite chic, piled with lacquered-red plates filled with food and centerpieces of gold bamboo containers holding exotic gold leaves.

Super-sized fortune cookies were a surprise for

A slew of Chinese parasols and close to a hundred red paper lanterns with black Chinese characters outfitted the room. Once I started to design the layout of the party, I realized how many lanterns I needed—the original thirty I had bought were a drop in the bucket compared to what I finally ended up spending to create my little fantasy for seventy people! I varied the heights of the hanging shades so they created the illusion of movement.

guests who had fun reading the messages we tucked inside.

This page: Long-stemmed palm leaves and fronds are secured in gold bamboo containers. When creating a centerpiece, I make sure guests can see each other across the table—otherwise, it's difficult to have a conversation.
Opposite page: Although it takes a little time to do, spray painting with gold offers impressive-looking decorations at very little cost.
Following pages: A behind-the-scenes peek at the preparations.

afternoon in Aspen

HIGH IN THE COLORADO ROCKIES,
A LUNCHEON TRANSPORTS GUESTS
TO AN ALPINE ADVENTURE.

I wanted to bring a touch of the Alps to the Rockies. Luckily, there was snow on the ground, and the weather complied: It was just warm enough for guests to feel comfortable outside on the porch. I slipped plaid wool blankets over the chairs in case guests felt chilly.

An awe-inspiring vista and bright daffodils

provide all the decoration needed for a memorable occasion.

Bright yellow daffodils evoke the coming of spring, which is a nice note to hit in a wintry landscape. At each place setting, I set a CD of Austrian music wrapped in striped paper and my signature saddle-stitched ribbon.

Skiing is one of my passions, and one of my fondest memories is learning to ski as a little girl in Switzerland and the get-togethers that would come after spending a day on the slopes. Here in the United States, we tend to head to the cafeteria after a run or two, but in my experience, Europeans have it right—they often eat outside in the open air, surrounded by snow-capped mountains and blue skies.

One day, I started thinking about how much fun it would be to host a party for my friends in Aspen instead of giving yet another dinner. The luncheon I planned had a lot to do with creating a lasting memory that lived up to the ones I treasured from my childhood. I remember the

crisp, fresh air, pristine slopes, and evergreen trees, as well as the décor of the lodge, what people wore, and the delicious food and drink that warmed us when we returned from a morning on the slopes.

This was the mood I wanted to evoke for my Austrian luncheon. The décor included evergreens and pinecones, as well as pewter dishes, stag-handled flatware, and beer steins. Guests came dressed in Nordic sweaters and Alpine jackets, and I served a delicious Hungarian Goulash (page 250) with spaetzle, red cabbage, and a large plate of cheeses, cornichons, and pretzels. For dessert, no one could resist the apple strudel with vanilla cream.

Guests joined in the spirit of the luncheon. Even though there was a wintry feeling, I used a palette of fresh shades of yellow and green for the party decorations as a counterpoint to the scenery around us.

Silver pewter beer steins and vases shine on a table set with moss-green linen tablecloths. A big bowl of Granny Smith apples makes an easy, striking centerpiece—a trick I often use when hard-pressed for fresh flowers or other decorations. Horn-handled utensils add texture to the place settings.

Snapshots from a memorable day, including Chef Michael Ruggeberg, who helped prepare a tasty buffet of Hungarian Goulash with spaetzle, red cabbage, delicious cheeses, and cornichons.

Ingenuity is part of the fun of planning a party—especially if time or resources are hard to come by. What would I do without my computer? It is so easy now to create beautiful invitations, menu cards, and place cards for a party, and I've found that these little touches mean a lot. I tied the invitations with a brown and white saddle-stitched ribbon and hand delivered them to my guests—and this same ribbon was used on gifts for each of them. It's this continuity of theme that helps create a memorable party. I love the color of Granny Smith apples, and I was lucky to be able to order masses of daffodils from the local grocery store to decorate the table.

the party process

Having an organized plan for a party goes a long way to ensuring a successful event.

The basics are the same, whether it's a ball or a dinner party, but to create something memorable and on a larger scale, the planning is more involved. In my opinion, the essence of a good dinner party boils down to three basic things; a relaxed and attentive host, good food, and the quality of the conversation of those attending. Anything else is the frosting on the cake.

There are two types of organizational lists to follow for Party Planning 101.

The first is what I call the left-brain list:
- Select a date
- Make a list of guests
- Call or mail an invitation
- Select a menu
- Determine if you need a caterer, cook, serving staff, or entertainment
- Send a reminder or call before the party to ensure guests are onboard
- Do the shopping for decorations and food
- Prepare the house and set the table
- Prepare the food and drinks
- Hosts get ready
- Guests arrive

The second type of organizational approach is the right-brain list. It is creative, and includes the same elements of the left-brain list but amplified several times over. I prepare that part of the party process by thinking of parties in the following way:

Occasion

Is there a specific reason for a party? A celebration of an event such as a wedding, birthday, anniversary, birth, graduation, the culmination of an important business deal, the launch of a new enterprise, an exhibition or showing of one's work (such as a collection of clothes, the publication of a book, the release of a recording), a recital, moving into a new home, a celebration of an important landmark or milestone in someone's life, the visit of family or friends from another place, or maybe you just feel like dancing—that has always been one of my favorite reasons. Maybe you want to reciprocate for the many invitations you've received, or you are simply so sad or so happy that you need to kick up your heels to have some fun.

There are endless reasons for having a party.

I am often motivated by the seasons, and of course, by the holidays. I like tradition because it provides stability and a sense of continuity to our lives. Sharing traditions with others is a wonderful thing.

I love the opportunity to celebrate the holidays, as it gives us a reason to let go of the everyday routine of our lives. I am certainly not complaining, as I have a wonderful life, but the truth is we all live lives, not of quiet desperation, but of responsibilities, commitments, deadlines, and a lot of little nitty-gritty things that are part of our daily existence. These are the necessities of life. Parties are not necessary, but life would get stale without them.

Nature and the change of the seasons has always been one of my major reasons for giving a party. To celebrate the blooming of a favorite flower in my garden—glorious peonies—was reason enough to celebrate with a spring dance. The autumn harvest and fall apple-picking, which heralds the onset of pies, cakes, crisps, and jellies can be a reason for a barn dance. Tomatoes and basil or the first sweet corn of the season is reason enough to celebrate. The list is endless.

Inspiration

There are millions of things that can inspire us to host a party. For example, my Chinese party was a result of a visit to Chinatown, where I found a slew of cheap red Chinese lanterns I loved. A beautiful snowfall inspired my New Year's Eve white dinner party; finding adorable birthday hats prompted me to do a kids' birthday party for a friend's child, and making a Halloween mask for my little friend Susanna energized the party for kids. Inspiration comes from a single color, a book, a piece of fabric, a tree, a movie, or travel. Inspiration comes from anything and everything, if our minds and our eyes are open.

So the reason and the inspiration come—and now what? I find that zeroing in upon a theme, motif, or a central idea is not only helpful in the party planning process but fun as well.

Creating a Theme

The difference between inspiration and the theme of a party is that the latter spells out in detail the inspiration. The theme allows us to produce what is in our minds—and make that fantasy come alive for others. It's similar to my thought process when I was a fashion designer creating a clothing collection. If violet and green were important colors in my fall line, then I would play with green and violet in many different ways, from daywear to evening clothes, to the accessories, to the lighting of the show, the press release, and even the invitation. The total presentation shouted this message. When the viewers left, they knew one thing for sure—that Carolyne Roehm's collection was about green and violet. The same thinking applies to parties. For Flower Power Fun, for example, I knew the bright, strong colors of the party hat were key. The little felt flowers on it prompted me to do the pillows and tablecloth in brightly colored felt and to decorate them with oversized felt flowers. The geometric forms and shapes on the hat led me to cut felt circles and add sequin circles everywhere. So bright colors, pop art flowers, and geometric shapes showed up on invitations and wrapping paper. Every detail of that party, including the food, was inspired by those little bright hats I had purchased three years earlier on a trip.

Back to Basics

We have the reason, the inspiration, and the theme. Now it is important to go back to the left-brain organization and make a list of the mechanics to bring these ideas into reality.

- Create a detailed guest list with pertinent information: address, home and office telephone numbers—that now includes cell phone numbers and e-mail addresses—proper salutation, and name of assistant, if applicable
- Create invitations based on the theme
- Mail invitations
- Make a list of products needed to decorate
- Make a list of necessary staff such as cooks, caterers, service staff, valet parking attendants, and then book those people for the date, establishing fees and working them into your budget
- Do the same for the entertainment. For example: For the Autumn Barn Dance, I needed to book fiddlers and dancers who would show the guests how to perform the basic do-si-dos
- If lighting is an issue, book a specialist for that
- If there are special flowers, trees, fabrics, party rentals such as chairs, tableware, tablecloths, and scenic props, research and order them in advance

Decoration

Once I determine the theme, I start planning the look of the party. The process is evolutionary—one idea creates another. Sometimes one idea can knock out another—this is the editing process of creativity. For example, when I bought my bargain Chinese lanterns with their red base and black Chinese characters, I decided to make the party all red and black. Working on the layout of the party at my studio one night (where the party was to be held), I decided that at night, the black would be too dead and that red and gold would be better to create the effect I wanted. From that point on, gold became the punctuation point in a sea of red. I sprayed the bamboo steamers gold and hung red Chinese good luck tassels on them and sprayed my centerpieces of exotic leaves gold. One should be flexible enough to change as one goes along.

At the beginning, I do a very rough sketch of how I want the room and the tables to look. This can also change, but it provides a simple blueprint for me as I go shopping for the elements I need. I do the same when I am decorating a room in a house. If a party has a lot of decorative details, I make lists of everything I need in order to create the look, such as paint, wire, transparent fishing line, and so on. The lists are quite long for the more involved parties, but by organizing and obtaining everything in advance, I make my life a lot easier.

Elements

This varies according to the theme and scale of the party. For a normal-sized dinner party, I use my own stemware, service, flatware, and linens. If the party is large, I must make arrangements for rentals such as glasses and chairs. I normally make my own tablecloths and napkins to ensure the integral look of my tables. I also tend to look for affordable plates and decorative glassware. For the Raise the Red Lanterns party, I found wonderful red lacquer plates that were chic and quite modern, and paired them with red lacquered chopsticks.

I made the tablecloths and bought the napkins and we made oversized lazy Susans for serving the food, spray-painting them lacquer red. The look was great! This is a matter of budget and available storage space, of course: I have collected so much stuff through the years that I keep threatening to have a tag sale someday.

Another important aspect is the lighting on the table. (The lighting of the room falls under decoration in my lists.) I have a large supply of classic and colored votives, but finding interesting candles such as tapers in unusual sizes and colors, pillars, hurricanes, and different candlesticks brings an important element to the look of the party.

For large parties, serving dishes become an issue. I have a set of oversized white serving dishes I have used over and over, but if they do not work, I will rent simple silver-plated trays, Revere bowls, and other serving pieces. I find that unornamented classic shapes work well with just about anything. They almost disappear and certainly do not distract from the look. I generally order classic wineglasses, glass plates or classic white ones, and very simple unornamented silver-plate flatware. These elements become neutral and do not interfere with the look I am trying to achieve.

Paper:
INVITATIONS, PLACECARDS, MENUS, REMINDERS, SAVE-THE-DATE CARDS

I love creating invitations. They are fun to do and are so important in setting the spirit and tone of a party. I always appreciate when someone makes the effort to do a special invitation—it increases my anticipation of the event. For the thematic parties, I do a coordinating invitation. For more traditional and smaller parties, I use my personal invitations. If my assistant calls in advance and the guest accepts, I will send a reminder card.

I normally do not use place cards for ten people or less—surely one can remember where that many people are to sit. The exception is if it is a special event like a baby shower and the place card is part of the table decoration. Likewise, I do not use menu cards for a small group. The exception to that is if the meal is created for special food—for example, during white truffle season or when special wines are being celebrated, then I think the party guests like to have the information.

For special parties, I usually pattern the menu card and the place cards after the invitation and the overall décor. For example, look at how red, white, and blue stripes of the Fourth of July party are echoed throughout the party, from the invitation to the fabric to the painted picnic tables and cotton napkins to the painted trays for the petit fours, to the flags (the inspiration) used as the centerpieces, to the place and menu cards, to the pastry stripes on the pie, and even my striped shirt! All of these elements using stripes in many sizes and mediums tie together to create the look of the party.

Food

I have studied food all of my life, taken many cooking courses, and planted my vegetable and herb gardens based upon the fresh foods I like to prepare and use as seasonings. And I love to eat. So food alone is a reason to give a dinner or a party in my book. When I have a theme such as the Chinese party, it is obvious that the food will be Chinese. But if the theme is a general spring celebration, then my food is based

upon the season and what is the freshest and the best for that time of year. The food that we prepare is old-fashioned comfort food because that is what I love. But when soft-shell crab or morels are in season, I make a special effort to do elegant food to use those luxurious ingredients.

With the plethora of cookbooks out there, we have access to endless ideas. My only word of caution is do not experiment with unknown recipes on guests—test the recipes on yourself first. Also try to look for certain dishes that may be cooked a day or two in advance. For example, coq au vin or a lamb ragu is always better when it is a couple of days old. There are numerous foods like that and it certainly helps to streamline preparations on the day of the party.

Extras: Gifts and Music

Depending on the occasion, I like to place little presents or favors at each guest's place. This can be anything from a CD, to a photo to commemorate the event, a special cookie or candy, a small book, or even a pretty plant. The other alternative is to give a little reminder of you or the evening when the guests depart, but this normally is for a holiday or a celebratory party, not a traditional dinner party.

Music is another key ingredient for any party, regardless of size. Music playing softly in a room relaxes the guests, while music that's a bit too loud becomes a nuisance. During dinner, I stay away from vocal music and stick to instrumental music, as I find it easier to talk over it to my dinner companions. Depending on the party and the activity, plan ahead whether you are booking a DJ or a live band for dancing, a pianist for cocktails, or musicians for Christmas caroling. Whatever the occasion, music is always a crucial element.

For additional help and ideas for a great party, go to www.carolyneroehm.com.

recipes

Chilled Fresh Pea Soup with Crab

This elegant cold soup has a little kick to it because of the jalapeño. If you like, you can add even more heat with a drop of hot chili oil.
Serves 6 to 8

4 tablespoons (½ stick) unsalted butter
¼ cup chopped shallots
1 large jalapeño pepper, seeds and ribs removed, chopped
6 cups chicken stock
6 cups fresh peas or three 10-ounce packages frozen peas
1 cup chopped fresh cilantro
1 teaspoon hot chili oil (optional)
Salt and freshly ground pepper
1 pound lump crabmeat, picked over for shells and cartilage

1 . In a large soup pot over medium heat, melt the butter and sauté the shallots and jalapeño until soft.
2 Add the chicken stock and peas and cook for 10 minutes. Turn off the heat and add the cilantro and hot oil, if using.
3 . Cool the mixture and puree it in a blender until smooth. Add salt and pepper to taste. Refrigerate the soup until very cold, 3 hours or more.
4 . Stir in the crabmeat and serve.

Poached Salmon with Cucumber Herb Sauce

If you're inviting more than eight guests, you may want to consider poaching a whole salmon that's been cleaned and scaled at the fish market. Be sure to also double the recipe for the Cucumber Herb Sauce, so you'll have plenty to go around.
Serves 6 to 8

One 3-inch piece fresh ginger, peeled and sliced
2 stalks lemongrass, crushed
2 to 3 bay leaves
1 cup dry white wine
1 tablespoon black peppercorns
8 salmon fillets (about 2 pounds)
Cucumber Herb Sauce (recipe follows)

1 . In a fish poacher or wide stockpot with a lid, make a court bouillon by combining 1 gallon of water with all the ingredients except the salmon. Simmer for 20 minutes, then turn off the heat and let the liquid cool for 10 minutes.
2 . Place the salmon in the court bouillon, bring to a simmer, and cook, covered, over low heat until the fish is just opaque, about 15 minutes. Remove the salmon, cool completely, and refrigerate.
3 . Serve with Cucumber Herb Sauce.

CUCUMBER HERB SAUCE
Most sauces for fish employ only one herb, such as basil or dill. I love this particular topping because of all the different flavors it combines, including the heat of red pepper flakes.
Makes 1 cup

⅔ cup coarsely chopped peeled cucumber
Salt
½ cup mayonnaise or whole milk yogurt
⅛ cup chopped fresh cilantro
⅛ cup chopped fresh flat-leaf parsley
⅛ cup chopped fresh dill
4 or 5 mint leaves
2 tablespoons fresh lemon juice
Pinch of salt
Pinch of red pepper flakes
⅛ cup extra virgin olive oil

1. Place the cucumber in a colander over the sink, salt well, and let sit for 1 hour to draw out excess water. Rinse well.

2. Place all the ingredients except for the olive oil in a blender or a food processor with the chopping blade attached and puree until smooth. Slowly add the olive oil with the machine running. The sauce will thicken slightly. Serve with poached salmon.

Angel Food Cake with Coconut Whipped Cream and Strawberries

Even calorie-conscious guests won't be able to turn down this temptation. If they do, persuade them to have a small bowl of berries and a thimbleful of the fluffy cream.
Serves 8

> 1 cup sifted Swans Down cake flour
> 1 cup confectioners' sugar
> 1½ cups egg whites
>   (12 to 14 large egg whites)
> ¼ teaspoon salt
> 1 teaspoon cream of tartar
> 1 cup granulated sugar
> ½ teaspoon almond extract
> 1 teaspoon vanilla extract
> Coconut Whipped Cream
>   (recipe follows)
> 2 pints fresh strawberries, stemmed and sliced
> 2 teaspoons fresh lemon juice

1. Preheat the oven to 425°F. Heat an ungreased 10-inch tube pan in the oven while making the batter.

2. Sift the flour and confectioners' sugar together into a medium bowl.

3. Combine the egg whites, salt, and cream of tartar in a large bowl and beat until foamy with an electric mixer at medium speed. Increase the speed to medium-high; beat until soft peaks form when the beaters are lifted. With the mixer running, sprinkle in the granulated sugar 2 tablespoons at a time, and beat until the egg whites stand in stiff peaks, but are not dry.

4. Using a rubber spatula or wire whisk, fold the flour mixture by tablespoons into the egg whites until all traces of flour disappear. Fold in the almond and vanilla extracts. Do not overmix.

5. Pour the batter into the hot tube pan. Bake for exactly 23 minutes, no longer. The cake should spring back when lightly touched. Invert the cake, still in the pan, on a metal funnel or a bottle; cool completely.

6. With a knife, carefully loosen the cake from the sides and center of the pan; invert onto a plate. Ice with Coconut Whipped Cream. Sprinkle the strawberries with lemon juice and serve in a glass bowl, if possible, alongside the cake.

COCONUT WHIPPED CREAM WITH LEMON ZEST

> 1½ cups heavy cream
> 1 cup sweetened shredded coconut
> 2 teaspoons lemon zest

Whip the cream on high speed with an electric mixer until stiff. Then gently fold in the coconut and lemon zest, using a rubber spatula or wire whisk.

BLOOMS DAY LUNCH

Chilled Zucchini Soup with Toasted Coconut

What I like about this cold, refreshing soup is its layers of flavor, from the ginger, garlic, and curry to the lime, mint, and coconut. Each spoonful is a surprise!
Serves 8

> 3 tablespoons extra virgin olive oil
> 2 cups chopped onion
> 1½ cups chopped celery
> 2 tablespoons chopped garlic
> 2 tablespoons chopped fresh ginger
> 3 tablespoons curry powder
> 6 cups chicken stock
> 6 medium zucchini, cut into 2-inch pieces
> One 14-oz can unsweetened coconut milk
> 1 tablespoon fresh lime juice
> 1 tablespoon chopped fresh mint
> Salt and freshly ground pepper
> ½ cup toasted coconut

1. In a soup pot, heat the olive oil over medium heat. Add the onion, celery, garlic, and ginger and sauté until soft. Add the curry powder and cook for 5 to 7 minutes, stirring until well combined.

2. Add the chicken stock and zucchini, and simmer until the zucchini is tender, 15 to 20 minutes.

3. Stir in the coconut milk, lime juice, and mint; let cool and carefully puree in a blender in batches until smooth.

4. Chill the soup until very cold: Season to taste with salt and pepper, then garnish with toasted coconut and serve.

Yellow Tomato Tartlets

The first harvest of the season delivers the most beautiful produce to use for an al fresco lunch. If yellow tomatoes aren't available, these mini tarts are just as delicious with red cherry tomatoes.
Serves 8

> Pie Crust (page 242), prepared through step 3
> 2 cups chopped scallions
> 1½ to 2 pounds yellow pear tomatoes, halved
> 1 pound goat cheese, crumbled
> 1 cup toasted sunflower seeds

1. Preheat the oven to 375°F. Lightly grease eight 4-inch tart pans.

2. Divide the dough into 8 equal pieces. Roll each portion into a 5-inch circle and transfer to the tart pans. Using your fingers, pat the dough evenly along the bottom and sides of the pan. Refrigerate the crusts for 30 minutes.

3. Place the tart pans on a baking sheet and bake for 10 minutes. Transfer to a wire rack and cool. Sprinkle approximately 2 tablespoons of scallions on the bottom of each pastry shell. Place the halved tomatoes on top of the scallions.

4. Put 4 or 5 teaspoons of goat cheese on top of the tomatoes in each tart. Sprinkle with the remaining scallions and the sunflower seeds and bake 20 to 25 minutes. Gently remove the tarts from the pans and serve immediately.

Heart-shaped Grilled Cheese Sandwiches

No child could resist this favorite sandwich in such a winning shape. For an adult version, spread a little spicy mustard on the inside of the bread before grilling.
Serves 8

> 8 tablespoons (1 stick) unsalted butter, softened
> 16 slices firm white bread or your favorite whole-grain bread, crusts removed
> Two 6-ounce packages sliced Vermont Cheddar cheese

1. Lightly grease a heart-shaped cookie cutter with butter. Make sandwiches, layering two slices of cheese inside and spreading softened butter on the outside of each slice of bread. Use the cookie cutter to cut out the sandwiches.
2. Heat a 10-inch nonstick skillet or nonstick griddle; add sandwiches; cover and cook over medium heat, carefully turning once, until golden brown on both sides and cheese melts.

NOTE: You can use any size cookie cutter, but I used a 3-inch heart, which yields one heart per sandwich. If you hate seeing the rest of the sandwich go to waste, cut out bite-size circles using the plastic screw-top from a water bottle.

Marinated Flank Steak

Lightly score the steak with a sharp knife before marinating, so the ingredients in this classic marinade infuse the beef. (It's easier to score the steak if you put it in the freezer for half an hour.) The sweetness of the maple syrup plays off the tang of the lemon juice and smokiness of the bourbon.
Serves 6

> 1 flank steak (1½ pounds)
> ½ cup finely chopped onion
> 3 garlic cloves, minced
> ½ cup ketchup
> ½ cup Worcestershire sauce
> 1 tablespoon Dijon mustard
> 1 tablespoon fresh lemon juice
> 2 tablespoons maple syrup
> 1 teaspoon freshly ground pepper
> ⅓ cup bourbon
> 2½ cups beef stock

1. Place the steak in the freezer for half an hour, then score the meat.
2. In a medium bowl, combine the onion, garlic, ketchup, Worcestershire, mustard, lemon juice, maple syrup, pepper, bourbon, and 1½ cups of the beef stock, and mix well.
3. Place the flank steak in a large shallow baking dish. Pour the mixture over the meat and marinate for 2 hours, turning occasionally. Remove the meat from the marinade; transfer the liquid to a saucepan and reserve.

4. Prepare a hot barbecue fire or grill and lightly oil the grill rack. Grill the steak over high heat, turning occasionally, 15 to 20 minutes for medium-rare. Transfer to a cutting board. Cover to keep warm and let stand 10 minutes.

5. Meanwhile, add the remaining cup of beef stock to the reserved marinade and boil for 10 minutes over medium-high heat.

6. Thinly slice the steak and arrange it on a serving platter. Pour the sauce over the slices and serve.

Farro Salad

An ancient grain that was used back in Roman times, farro (pronounced *FAHR-oh*) has made its mark at fancy restaurants in soups, salads, and even desserts. If you're unable to find it at your local grocery store, you can substitute the more familiar wheat berry or spelt in this recipe.
Serves 10 to 12

> 1 pound farro, cooked according to
>   package directions
> 1 small red onion, diced
> 1 red pepper, diced
> 1 yellow pepper, diced
> 1 zucchini, diced
> 1 yellow squash, diced
> 2 cups loosely packed arugula
> 2 tablespoons chopped fresh mint
> ½ cup chopped fresh chives
> ½ cup chopped fresh basil
> Vinaigrette (recipe follows)
> Salt and freshly ground pepper

Combine all of the ingredients in a medium serving bowl; toss with Vinaigrette. Season to taste with salt and pepper.

VINAIGRETTE
Makes 2 cups

> 2 garlic cloves, minced
> 1 shallot, minced
> 1 tablespoon Dijon mustard
> ¼ cup apple cider vinegar
> ¾ cup extra virgin olive oil

Whisk together all the ingredients until emulsified.

FOURTH OF JULY PARTY

Barbecued Baby Back Ribs

Most people think rhubarb is a fruit, but it's actually classified as a vegetable. Along with the brown sugar and orange juice, it sweetens the sticky sauce for these summertime ribs.
Serves 6

> 4½ to 5 pounds of baby back pork ribs (3 slabs)
> Rhubarb Barbecue Sauce (recipe follows)

1. Divide each slab of ribs in half and smear each piece with the sauce. Seal in a plastic bag and marinate in the refrigerator 4 to 6 hours, or longer if you want to start the marinade the night before the party.

2. Prepare a medium-hot barbecue grill or fire. Lightly oil the grill rack. Grill the ribs, turning occasionally, until browned and crusty, about 40 minutes.

RHUBARB BARBECUE SAUCE

This delectable sauce can be used on ribs or chicken.
Makes 2 cups

> 3 tablespoons extra virgin olive oil
> 1 medium onion, chopped
> One 2-inch piece fresh ginger, peeled and finely chopped
> 6 garlic cloves, finely chopped
> ¾ pound rhubarb, cut into ½-inch pieces (2 cups)
> ½ cup dark brown sugar
> ½ cup soy sauce
> ½ cup orange juice
> 1 teaspoon Thai chili paste (optional)

1. In a medium saucepan, heat the olive oil. Sauté the onion, ginger, and garlic over medium heat for 3 minutes.

2. Add the rhubarb, brown sugar, soy sauce, and orange juice. Add chili paste to taste, if using. Cook over medium-low heat, stirring frequently, for 20 minutes. Cool and puree in a blender or food processor.

Zesty Baked Beans

In New England, B&M has been famous for its brick oven baked beans since 1867. I've made my own fiery version for many years at Weatherstone. No one will know you started with a couple of cans of beans. The few other ingredients add a huge amount of extra flavor.

Serves 6

> 1 pound bacon
> 1 large onion, coarsely chopped
> 1 jalapeño pepper, finely chopped
> Two 32-ounce cans B&M Original Baked Beans
> ¼ cup maple syrup
> 1 teaspoon ground chipotle pepper
> 2 tablespoons Worcestershire sauce

1. Preheat the oven to 350°F.

2. Cut the bacon into 1-inch pieces. In a deep frying pan over medium heat, brown the bacon until crisp. Drain on a paper towel, reserving ¼ cup of the fat in the pan.

3. Heat the reserved bacon fat, and sauté the onion and jalapeño pepper until the onion is golden.

4. Add the beans, maple syrup, chipotle pepper, and Worcestershire sauce to the pan, and mix well.

5. Pour the bean mixture into an ovenproof dish. Bake uncovered for 45 minutes and serve.

Sour Cherry Pie

I love the taste of tart sour cherries and wish they were available longer than the two or three weeks in June when you can buy them fresh at the farm stand. I sometimes buy extra and freeze them to prolong the season. Whenever you serve it, cherry pie is a special treat for guests, who invariably ask for a second slice.

Serves 8

> Double recipe for Pie Crust (page 242), prepared
>   through step 3, or two 9-inch store-bought pie crusts
> 4 cups fresh sour cherries, pitted
> 1½ cups sugar
> 2½ tablespoons quick-cooking tapioca
> 3 tablespoons amaretto

1. Preheat the oven to 450°F.

2. On a lightly floured surface, roll half the dough to a 12-inch round. Fit the dough into a 9-inch glass pie pan, pressing into the edges. Trim the dough to meet the edge of the pan. Prick the bottom of the dough with a fork.

3. Mix all the ingredients and pour them into the prepared pie crust. Roll out the rest of the dough on wax paper and, using a serrated knife or roller, cut three ½-inch by 9-inch strips. Use a miniature star-shaped cookie cutter to make 25 to 30 stars. Lay the strips—the "stripes" to go with the stars—across the pie and place the stars around the edges and on top.

4. Bake at 450°F for 15 minutes. Reduce the heat to 350°F and bake for an additional 30 to 40 minutes, or until the crust is golden. Cool on a wire rack and serve.

SUNFLOWER SOIRÉE

Jambalaya

The name itself has a festive sound, and this New Orleans dish, which is sometimes likened to paella, looks great on the table with its green peppers, red tomatoes, and pale pink shrimp.
Serves 12

¼ cup extra virgin olive oil
2 boneless, skinless chicken breasts,
   cut into 2-inch pieces
2½ cups chopped onion
8 garlic cloves, chopped
2 cups chopped celery
2 cups chopped green pepper
2 jalapeño peppers, seeds and ribs removed, chopped
3 tablespoons dried thyme
2 pounds andouille sausage, cut into 2-inch pieces
One 12-ounce can plum tomatoes with juice
6 cups chicken stock
2 teaspoons salt
3 cups long-grain rice
2 pounds medium shrimp, peeled and deveined
1 cup chopped scallions
1 cup chopped fresh flat-leaf parsley
1 cup chopped fresh tomato
Salt and freshly ground pepper

1. Preheat the oven to 375°F.

2. In a deep cast-iron Dutch oven or stainless steel pot, heat the olive oil and brown the chicken, but do not cook it completely. Remove the chicken and set aside.

3. In the same pan, sauté the onion, garlic, celery, green and jalapeño peppers, and thyme until soft.

4. Add the sausage and sauté for 2 minutes. Crush the canned tomatoes with your hands and add with the juice; add the chicken stock and salt and simmer for 15 minutes.

5. Stir in the rice and mix well. Cover and place in the oven for 30 minutes.

6. When the rice is almost done, add the chicken and shrimp; cover and return to the oven for 10 to 15 minutes.

7. Remove from the oven and fold in the scallions, parsley, and fresh tomato. Add salt and pepper to taste. Serve immediately.

Crisp Radish Salad

Refreshing and low in calories, since it is made without oil, this easy-to-transport radish salad won't wilt like one made with lettuce and can be made a day in advance.
Serves 6

> 24 fresh radishes, trimmed, washed, thinly sliced
> 1 cup rice vinegar
> 6 tablespoons mirin (sweet rice wine available in
>   Japanese or specialty markets)
> 1 cup chopped fresh cilantro
> Salt and freshly ground pepper

Place all the ingredients in a bowl. Toss, adjust the seasoning to taste, and serve.

SESAME DIPPING SAUCE

> ¼ cup toasted sesame seeds
> ¼ cup tamari sauce
> ¼ cup extra virgin olive oil
> ¼ cup rice vinegar
> 1 tablespoon chopped fresh ginger
> 1 teaspoon hot chili oil
> 1 teaspoon sugar
> 1 garlic clove

Place all ingredients in a blender and puree until smooth.

Shrimp Spring Rolls

The ingredient list for these light, tasty spring rolls may seem daunting, but in truth, the prep work goes quickly.
Makes 12 rolls

> 12 rice paper wrappers
> 24 medium cooked shrimp (about 2 pounds),
>   peeled, deveined, and sliced in half lengthwise
> 2 cups shredded red or green leaf lettuce
> 1½ cups shredded carrots
> 6 scallions, root ends and tops trimmed,
>   sliced lengthwise
> 4 ounces enoki mushrooms (optional)
> 3 ounces vermicelli rice noodles, soaked in
>   boiling water for 10 minutes, drained
> ¼ cup chopped fresh mint
> ¼ cup chopped fresh basil
> ¼ cup chopped fresh cilantro
> 1 bunch of chives for garnish
> Sesame Dipping Sauce (preceding recipe)

1. Soak the wrappers one at a time for 30 seconds in warm water or until soft. Shake off excess water and put the wrapper on a plate. As you use one wrapper, soak the next.
2. Working quickly, place 2 shrimp halves end to end in the middle of a wrapper. Place a small amount of each of the remaining ingredients—lettuce, carrots, scallions, mushrooms (if using), noodles, mint, basil, and cilantro—on top, finishing with 2 more shrimp halves. Fold the bottom of the wrapper over the filling, fold in the sides, and then fold over the top to complete the roll. Repeat with the remaining wrappers to make 12 rolls. Cover with damp paper towels until ready to serve.
3. Decorate with chives and serve with Sesame Dipping Sauce.

Lemon Curd Tartlets

After a lunch with spicy and salty elements, a cool, citrusy dessert seems like the perfect ending.

Serves 6

Tartlet Shells (recipe follows)
3 large eggs
⅓ cup fresh lemon juice
¾ cup granulated sugar
4 tablespoons (½ stick) unsalted butter,
    cut into pieces
2 tablespoons lemon zest

1. In a double boiler, whisk together the eggs, lemon juice and sugar until blended. Cook over simmering water, whisking constantly, until the mixture becomes pale and quite thick, about 10 minutes.
2. Remove from heat and pour through a fine sieve. Whisk in the butter pieces until melted.
3. Add the zest; cool completely. Pour the curd into the large tart or tartlet shells no more than 2 hours before serving.

TARTLET SHELLS

1½ cups all-purpose flour
12 tablespoons (1½ sticks) cold unsalted butter,
    cut into small pieces
5 tablespoons confectioners' sugar

1. Preheat the oven to 350°F.
2. Place all ingredients in the bowl of a food processor and pulse until the mixture is crumbly. Press lightly into a 9-inch tart pan or six 3-inch tartlet pans. Bake approximately 20 minutes (8 to 10 minutes for small tarts) or until golden. Cool before removing from the pans.

AUTUMN BARN DANCE

Smothered Chicken

Smothered chicken is an American classic, by way of the South, with innumerable versions. The one constant (other than the poultry!) is flour, which contributes to the light gravy that smothers the browned chicken. You'll want to make a lot because everyone always clamors for more.

Serves 6

One 6-pound chicken, cut into 8 pieces,
    rinsed and patted dry
Salt and freshly ground pepper
3 tablespoons all-purpose flour
3 tablespoons extra virgin olive oil
2 tablespoons unsalted butter
1 medium onion, minced
1 cup sliced mushrooms
2 garlic cloves, minced
1 tablespoon curry powder
½ cup dry sherry
1 cup white wine
1 bay leaf
1 tablespoon chopped fresh flat-leaf parsley
2 cups chicken broth

1. Season the chicken with salt and pepper. Dredge the pieces in flour, shaking off the excess.
2. Heat 2 tablespoons of the oil in a large skillet over medium heat. Add the chicken, skin side down, and cook, turning once, until light golden. Remove and set aside.

3. In a Dutch oven, heat the remaining tablespoon of oil and the butter over medium heat. Add the onion and sauté until golden, about 2 minutes.

4. Add the mushrooms and garlic, and sauté for 5 minutes.

5. Add the curry, sherry, and wine, and boil for 5 minutes.

6. Add the bay leaf, parsley, and chicken broth, and continue boiling for 5 minutes.

7. Add the chicken and cover, simmering for 30 to 45 minutes over. Transfer to a serving platter. Serve immediately.

Garlic and Rosemary Potatoes

You couldn't ask for a better crowd-pleaser. Use any kind of potato—fingerling, Yukon Gold, new, or Idaho.
Serves 6

> 3 tablespoons unsalted butter
> 2½ pounds potatoes, peeled and sliced ¼ inch thick
> 6 garlic cloves, sliced
> 3 tablespoons chopped fresh rosemary
> Salt and freshly ground pepper
> 2 to 3 tablespoons extra virgin olive oil
> ½ cup chicken stock

1. Preheat the oven to 375°F.

2. Butter a 9 x 13-inch ovenproof pan with 1 tablespoon of the butter.

3. Cover the bottom of the pan with a third of the potatoes, sprinkle on a third of the garlic and rosemary, and dot the layer with 1 tablespoon of butter. Add salt and pepper to taste. Continue layering until you complete three layers.

4. Drizzle the top layer with the olive oil and pour in the chicken stock. Cover with foil and bake for 30 minutes.

5. Remove the foil and continue baking for 15 minutes or until the top is golden and the potatoes are cooked. Remove from the oven and serve.

Bread Pudding with Bourbon Sauce

Challah is my bread of choice for this comfort-food dessert, but brioche or French or Italian bread will work also. A rich bourbon sauce is the perfect topping.
Serves 10 to 12

> 1-pound loaf challah bread, slightly stale,
>   cut into 1-inch cubes
> 4 cups whole milk
> 1½ cups golden raisins
> ½ cup bourbon
> 5 large eggs
> ½ cup heavy cream
> 1½ cups sugar
> 2 tablespoons vanilla extract
> 1 teaspoon cinnamon
> Bourbon Sauce (recipe follows)

1. Preheat the oven to 325°F. Butter a 9 x 13 x 2-inch nonreactive baking pan.

2. In a large shallow baking dish, soak the bread in the milk for 15 to 30 minutes. In a small bowl, soak the raisins in the bourbon for 15 to 30 minutes.

3. Combine the eggs, cream, sugar, vanilla, and cinnamon in a large bowl; beat well. Using a spatula, transfer the soaked bread to the buttered pan. Pour the egg mixture and raisins over the bread.

4. Bake for 1 hour and 10 minutes.

5. Remove from the oven; serve with Bourbon Sauce.

BOURBON SAUCE
Makes 1 cup

4 tablespoons (½ stick) unsalted butter
1 cup confectioners' sugar
½ cup heavy cream
¼ cup bourbon

1. Melt the butter in a small saucepan over medium heat. Add the sugar; stir until combined.
2. Add the cream and whisk until smooth. Remove from heat. Stir in the bourbon; let cool.

Pumpkin Pie

For an autumn party, I like to serve this maple-syrup-and-rum-spiked pumpkin pie created by Nancy Quantrini, Weatherstone's cook for all seasons. A bit more nutmeg along with the rum gives our version of this classic Thanksgiving staple a little edge.
Serves 8

Pie Crust (recipe follows), prepared through step 5
½ teaspoon ground cinnamon
½ teaspoon ground nutmeg
½ teaspoon ground ginger
½ teaspoon salt
2 large eggs, beaten
¾ cup heavy cream
¾ cup sugar
One 15-ounce can pumpkin
¼ cup maple syrup
2 tablespoons Captain Morgan rum

1. Prepare the Pie Crust. Preheat the oven to 450°F.
2. Combine the cinnamon, nutmeg, ginger, and salt in a small bowl.
3. In a separate bowl, beat the eggs, cream, and sugar. Mix in the pumpkin, maple syrup, rum, and spices.
4. Pour the mixture into the prepared pie crust and bake at 450°F for 15 minutes. Reduce heat to 350°F, and continue baking for 50 to 60 minutes, or until the filling is firm in the center. Transfer to a wire rack to cool.

PIE CRUST
Makes one 9-inch crust

1¼ cups all-purpose flour
Pinch of salt
8 tablespoons (1 stick) cold unsalted butter,
   cut into small pieces
2 to 3 tablespoons ice water

1. Combine flour and salt in the bowl of a food processor; pulse 3 times to blend. Add the butter; pulse about 8 times to distribute butter until the dough resembles small peas.
2. Add ice water gradually by tablespoons through the feed tube, pulsing until the dough begins to pull together into a ball. Do not process more than 30 seconds. If the mixture is too crumbly, add a bit more water, 1 tablespoon at a time.
3. Remove the dough, shape it into a disk, sprinkle lightly with flour, and wrap in wax paper. Refrigerate until ready to roll out for pie.
4. On a lightly floured surface, roll the dough to a 12-inch round. Fit the dough into a 9-inch glass pie pan, pressing into the edges. Trim the dough to meet the edge of the pan. Prick the bottom of the dough with a fork.

Sesame Chicken Fingers with Peach Honey Sauce

These chicken fingers will seem happily familiar to children, and grown-ups will be intrigued by the Asian touches of panko (Japanese bread crumbs) and sesame seeds.
Serves 6

> 2 whole boneless, skinless chicken breasts,
>   cut into ½-inch-thick slices
> ¾ cup whole milk
> ½ cup sesame seeds
> 1 cup panko
> 2 teaspoons salt
> 1 teaspoon freshly ground pepper
> Cooking oil for frying
> Peach Honey Sauce (recipe follows)

1. Soak the chicken in milk in a large shallow dish.

2. Mix the sesame seeds, panko, salt, and pepper together in a pie plate.

3. In a nonstick frying pan, heat the oil over medium-high heat. Remove the chicken slices from the milk and coat with the breading mixture. Cook the chicken in small batches until the "fingers" are golden brown, approximately 2 minutes on each side. Arrange on a platter and serve with Peach Honey Sauce.

NOTE: If you're unable to find panko at your local grocery store, you can get them online at www.bakerscatalogue.com, or simply use plain dried bread crumbs.

PEACH HONEY SAUCE

Ketchup is the condiment of choice for most kids, but little ones may find themselves switching midparty to this sweet concoction.
Makes about ½ cup

> ¼ cup peach marmalade
> 1 tablespoon Dijon mustard
> 1 tablespoon honey

Mix ingredients together and serve with Sesame Chicken Fingers.

Cookie-Cutter French Fries

Imagine the delight of eating a French fry shaped like a bat, a jack o' lantern, or a witch's hat! Make a big batch for your trick-or-treat party guests.
Serves 4

> 1½ pounds Idaho or red potatoes, peeled
> Cooking oil (enough to cover the potato slices)
> ½ teaspoon salt

1. Slice the potatoes ¼-inch thick and cut out shapes with Halloween cookie cutters.

2. In a nonstick skillet, heat the oil over medium-high heat and deep-fry the potatoes until they are golden and puffy. Remove with a spatula and drain on paper towels. Sprinkle with salt and serve.

Gravlax with Crème Fraîche and Mustard

I like the pungent aroma of the spices in this beloved appetizer. Each time I prepare it, I marvel at how simple gravlax is to make. And as someone who is keen on color, I find the pretty coral of the salmon particularly appealing.
Serves 12 to 24

> 2 to 3 pounds wild salmon fillet, tail end, skin on
> 2 tablespoons juniper berries
> 2 tablespoons mixed peppercorns
> 1 tablespoon fennel seeds
> 2 cups sugar
> 1½ cups kosher salt
> 2 bunches fresh dill
> ¾ cup gin, vodka, or tequila
> Brown bread, for serving
> Crème fraîche, for serving
> Dijon mustard, for serving

1. Place the salmon in a large glass or stainless steel roasting pan.
2. Crush the juniper berries, peppercorns, and fennel seeds with a mortar and pestle or coarsely grind in a coffee grinder. Sprinkle over the salmon.
3. In a small bowl, mix the sugar and salt and pour evenly over the salmon.
4. Place dill on top of the salmon.
5. Pour the gin over the salmon; cover with plastic wrap and place a weight on top. (I use a small cutting board with something heavy on it.)
6. Refrigerate for at least 3 days and up to 2 weeks.

7. Remove the salmon and scrape off the seasonings. Slice the salmon on an angle as thinly as possible, about ⅛ inch thick. Serve with 1½-inch squares of brown bread and small bowls of crème fraîche and Dijon mustard.

Prosciutto-wrapped Cherry Tomatoes in Parmesan Cups

Once you've mastered this appetizer, it will seem like the easiest, most elegant hors d'oeuvre to serve when you're entertaining.
Serves 6

> 1 cup grated Parmesan cheese
> 1 pint cherry tomatoes
> ½ pound prosciutto, sliced thin and
>   cut into ½-inch strips

1. Preheat the oven to 350°F. Line a cookie sheet with parchment paper.
2. Place tablespoonfuls of cheese on the cookie sheet, 1 inch apart. Bake until golden, approximately 8 minutes.
3. Working quickly and carefully, because the cheese is light and fragile at this point, remove the Parmesan pieces with a spatula and press gently into the cups of a nonstick mini muffin tin to form the Parmesan cups.
4. Wrap each tomato with a piece of prosciutto and place in a cup, seam side down. Once the Parmesan has hardened, about 10 minutes, remove from the muffin tins, place on a platter, and serve.

Mini Lemon Crêpes Stuffed with Lobster

This batter is a true all-around basic. You can use it for dessert crêpes filled with berries. For a late-night supper, this recipe is lovely—just make the crepes larger.
Serves 10

CRÊPE BATTER
1½ cups sifted all-purpose flour
2 eggs, beaten
Pinch of salt
½ cup milk
2 tablespoons melted butter
1 teaspoon grated lemon rind

LOBSTER FILLING
1½ cups chopped lobster meat
½ cup finely chopped celery
1 teaspoon grated onion
1 tablespoon Dijon mustard
3 tablespoons crème fraîche
1 tablespoon chopped fresh tarragon
Salt and pepper to taste
Chives for tying

1 . *For the crêpe batter:* In a medium bowl, mix the sifted flour, eggs, and salt together. Set aside.

2 . In a small bowl, mix the milk and ½ cup water together and gradually pour into the batter while mixing with a wire whisk or fork.

3 . Whisk in the butter and lemon rind and mix until smooth. Cover the bowl and refrigerate the batter for 2 hours.

4 . *For the lobster filling:* Mix all of the ingredients together in a medium bowl. Set aside.

5 . To make the crêpes: Heat a crêpe pan or griddle over medium-high heat until a drop of water evaporates on contact. Pour crêpe mixture into pan, forming circles that are approximately 3½ to 4 inches in diameter. Cook for 1 to 2 minutes. Flip once and remove from heat.

6 . Place 1 heaping teaspoon of filling in each crêpe and spread it evenly over the crêpe. Roll up the crêpe and tie it with a chive. Makes 20 to 30 hors d'oeuvres.

Mini BLTs

Classic bacon, lettuce, and tomato sandwiches cut into small hors d'oeuvre–size portions are a fun and satisfying appetizer at a cocktail party—and easy to make, too.
Makes 96

1 loaf firm white bread
12 large, firm tomatoes
Salt and freshly ground pepper
1 pound bacon
Mayonnaise
2 bunches flat-leaf parsley, finely chopped

1 . Preheat the oven to 350°F.

2 . To make the small toasts, use a 1-inch biscuit cutter to cut rounds from the slices of bread. (You'll be able to make almost 100 rounds from one loaf.) Bake on a sheet pan in the oven for 10 minutes turning halfway through until golden on both sides.

3 . Slice the tomatoes about the same thickness as the toast. Lay the slices on a paper towel to dry, season with salt, and grind the fresh pepper over them.

4 . Heat a large frying pan and cook the bacon over medium heat until crisp. Drain on paper towels, then chop or crumble into very fine pieces by hand.

5 . Spread a thin layer of mayonnaise on one side of the toast rounds. Place a slice of tomato on top, spread more mayonnaise on the tomato, and place a teaspoon of crumbled bacon on top. Sprinkle with parsley and serve. The BLTs can be made 2 hours in advance and kept at room temperature.

A HOLIDAY TRADITION

Spiced Sugar Cookies

Everyone has a favorite holiday sugar cookie recipe, and I'm no exception. This one stands out because of the extra cinnamon. For a cookie-decorating party, make several batches of Royal Icing in different colors, so children have lots of choices.
Makes about 3 dozen

> 3 cups all-purpose flour
> ¾ pound (3 sticks) unsalted butter,
>   cut into small pieces
> 1½ cups light brown sugar
> 1 teaspoon salt
> 2 tablespoons milk, or more as needed
> 1 tablespoon ground cinnamon
> 1 teaspoon ground cloves
> 1 teaspoon ground nutmeg
> Royal Icing (recipe follows)

1. Preheat the oven to 350°F. Lightly grease a cookie sheet.
2. Combine all ingredients except the icing in a large bowl. Knead with your fingers until all ingredients are well mixed. Add more milk if necessary to form into a ball. Wrap the dough in wax paper and chill for 1 hour.
3. Roll the dough about ⅛-inch thick. Cut with cookie cutters and place on the prepared cookie sheet. Bake for 8 to 10 minutes or until browned. Cool on wire racks. Ice with Royal Icing.

ROYAL ICING

This recipe makes extra, so that you can divide the icing into different colored batches. If you cannot find meringue powder at your grocer, look for it in specialty baking and gourmet shops.
Makes 3 cups

> 3 tablespoons meringue powder
> 4 cups confectioners' sugar
> Food coloring (optional)

Combine the meringue powder and confectioners' sugar in a large bowl. Using an electric mixer, beat in 5 tablespoons warm water until the icing forms peaks, about 10 minutes. If the icing is too stiff, beat in another tablespoon of water. Divide in to different bowls, depending on the colors you want, and add food coloring, if desired.

CHRISTMAS EVE AT WEATHERPEBBLE

Glazed Veal Chops

On Christmas Eve, a small group of us sat down to a quiet, elegant dinner. My choice for a main course was veal, which cooks quickly with minimal effort. For moist and tender chops, be sure not to cook the meat beyond medium. Demi-glace, which is reduced beef or veal stock, can be purchased at gourmet shops.
Serves 6

> 6 veal chops, 1½ inches thick
> Salt and freshly ground pepper
> 2 tablespoons extra virgin olive oil
> ½ cup red wine
> 1 teaspoon veal demi-glace

1. Season the veal chops with salt and pepper. Heat the olive oil in a large frying pan over medium-high heat. Sear the veal chops for 5 minutes or until browned.
2. Reduce the heat to medium; turn the chops and continue cooking for 8 to 10 minutes, until medium rare.
3. Transfer the chops to a serving platter and cover to keep warm.
4. Turn the heat to high, add the red wine, and reduce by half. Add 1 cup water and the demi-glace and reduce to ⅓ cup. Pour the glaze over the chops and serve.

Braised Endive

You may not have heard of Treviso, but like endive, it's a member of the chicory family. Both are slightly bitter, but after cooking in a bit of butter and chicken stock, each has its own less assertive, distinctive flavor. Either is the perfect foil for the richness of the veal.
Serves 6

> 3 tablespoons unsalted butter
> 1½ pounds Belgian endive or Treviso, trimmed and halved
> 1 cup chicken stock
> Salt and freshly ground pepper

1. In a large frying pan, melt the butter over medium-high heat. Add the endive, cut side down, in a single layer. Sauté for about 5 minutes; turn and sauté the other side for 2 minutes.
2. Reduce the heat to low; add the chicken stock and salt and pepper to taste. Cover and cook for 20 to 30 minutes or until tender. Transfer to a warm platter and serve.

Puree of Squash with Fried Sage Butter

Sage is an herb that is strongly associated with the holidays, from its seasoning of Thanksgiving stuffing to its role in this delicious accompaniment.
Serves 6

> 5 tablespoons unsalted butter
> 2½-pound butternut squash, peeled, seeded, and cut into ½-inch pieces
> ½ cup vegetable broth
> Salt and freshly ground pepper
> 2 tablespoons coarsely chopped fresh sage.

1. Melt 2 tablespoons of the butter in a large saucepan over medium heat. Add the squash, cover, and cook for 5 minutes.
2. Pour in the broth and simmer until the squash is soft, about 12 minutes. Let cool.
3. Working in batches, puree the squash in a blender or food processor until smooth. Season with salt and pepper to taste. Return the squash to the pan and reheat.
4. In a small saucepan, melt the remaining 3 tablespoons butter over medium heat. Add the sage and cook for 1 to 2 minutes. Pour over the squash and serve.

Cornish Game Hens

At Christmastime, a simple but elegant meal can be a relief after the cocktails and canapés, sweets and savories, and over-the-top entrees one eats during the holidays. This recipe is easy to make and dramatic to present.

Serves 2 to 4

> 2 Cornish game hens (1 ½ pounds each)
> 12 red or green seedless grapes
> 2 sprigs fresh tarragon
> 2 tablespoons extra virgin olive oil
> 1 tablespoon fresh thyme leaves
> Salt and freshly ground pepper

1. Preheat the oven to 450°F.

2. Remove the giblets and necks from the hens; reserve for another use or discard. Rinse the hens inside and out with cold running water and drain well. Pat dry with paper towels.

3. Stuff each of the hens with half the grapes and a sprig of tarragon.

4. Rub each bird with 1 tablespoon of olive oil. Sprinkle with fresh thyme, salt, and pepper.

5. Place the hens, breast side up, on a rack in a small roasting pan and cook for 15 minutes. Lower the heat to 350°F and continue roasting for 20 to 30 minutes, basting frequently, until the hens are tender and juices run clear when the thickest part of the thigh is pierced with the tip of a knife.

6. Remove the pan from oven, arrange the hens on a platter, and serve.

Wild Mushroom Risotto Cake

Dried wild mushrooms deliver an extra dose of earthy flavor to the fresh ones in this substantial side dish. Many people think risotto is difficult to get right, but all you need to do is be consistent in adding more broth—and keep stirring as the rice absorbs it. The great thing about this dish is that you can make the risotto a few hours ahead and keep it in the refrigerator until you are ready to bake the cake.

Serves 8 to 10

> 1 ounce dried porcini or other wild mushrooms
> 4 tablespoons olive oil
> 1 pound fresh portobello and/or shiitake
>   mushrooms, chopped, tough stems removed
> 2 quarts chicken stock
> 1 ½ medium shallots, coarsely chopped
> 2 ½ cups Arborio (Italian short-grain) rice
> 1 ¼ teaspoons salt
> 1 ¼ teaspoon freshly ground pepper
> 1 cup dry white wine
> 3 tablespoons unsalted butter
> 1 ½ cups grated Parmesan cheese
> 2 tablespoons chopped fresh tarragon

1. Soak the dried mushrooms in 1 ½ cups hot water for 15 to 20 minutes. Remove the mushrooms, reserving the broth; strain the broth through cheesecloth and set aside.

2. Heat 2 tablespoons of the olive oil in a frying pan; sauté the fresh mushrooms and set aside.

3. In a large saucepan, heat the reserved mushroom broth and the chicken stock and keep at a simmer.

4. In a 4-quart saucepan, heat the remaining 2 tablespoons olive oil over medium-high heat. Sauté the shallots until golden, about 5 minutes. Add the rice and season with salt and pepper, stirring until the rice grains are opaque.

5. Add the wine; cook until the wine has been absorbed. Add about ½ cup of the simmering broth to the rice, stirring until the liquid has been absorbed. Continue cooking, adding the remaining broth ½ cup at a time and stirring after each addition, until all liquid has been absorbed and the rice is tender but still firm, about 25 minutes. The rice should have a creamy consistency. Add more liquid if necessary, as it will absorb in baking.

6. Stir in the fresh and dried mushrooms, butter, 1 cup of the Parmesan cheese, and tarragon. Preheat oven to 350°F.

7. Butter a 9-inch springform pan. Place the risotto in the prepared pan and bake for 30 to 40 minutes. Remove from the pan and place on a platter. Sprinkle with the remaining Parmesan cheese and serve.

Poached Pears Wrapped in Pastry

Although the poaching liquid was developed in the Weatherstone kitchen, I got the idea for wrapping pears in pastry from the renowned French chef Paul Bocuse.

Serves 6

2⅓ cups port

2⅓ cups orange juice

½ cup plus 1 tablespoon granulated sugar

Two 3-inch cinnamon sticks

6 whole cloves

6 black peppercorns

One 3-inch strip lemon zest

6 ripe Bosc pears, peeled, stems intact

PASTRY

4 cups all-purpose flour

½ teaspoon salt

8 tablespoons (1 stick) cold unsalted butter,
   cut into small pieces

½ cup cold vegetable shortening,
   cut into small pieces

2 large eggs

1 tablespoon heavy cream

1. In a large nonreactive saucepan, combine 2⅓ cups water, the port, orange juice, and ½ cup of the sugar. Stir over medium heat until the sugar dissolves.

2. Add the cinnamon sticks, cloves, peppercorns, and lemon zest. Reduce heat to medium-low and simmer for 15 minutes. Add the pears and poach covered 15 to 25 minutes, depending on the ripeness of the fruit, until tender but not mushy.

3. Allow the pears to cool in the pan. Place the pears and liquid in a bowl, cover with plastic wrap, and refrigerate overnight.

4. To make the pastry dough, combine the flour, remaining tablespoon of sugar, and salt in the bowl of a food processor and pulse about 3 times to blend. Add the butter and shortening and pulse about 8 times, until the mixture resembles small peas.

5. Lightly beat 1 egg in a small bowl, add it to the flour mixture, and pulse several times. Add 4 to 6 tablespoons ice water through the feed tube gradually, by the tablespoon, while pulsing the machine. When you've added enough water, the dough will begin to come together into a ball. Remove the dough from the processor, divide in half, and shape into 2 disks. Sprinkle the dough lightly with flour and wrap in plastic wrap. Refrigerate for at least 2 hours.

6. When you are ready to assemble the pears, preheat the oven to 375°F. Grease a baking sheet.

7. Remove the pears from their poaching liquid and set aside. Strain the liquid into a medium saucepan and bring to a boil. Reduce the heat to medium and simmer briskly, uncovered, until reduced by half; set aside.

8. While the liquid is reducing, lightly beat the remaining egg and the cream in a small bowl until blended; set aside. Roll each disk of dough into a ⅛-inch-thick rectangle measuring 13½ x 8 inches; trim dough as needed. Using a pastry wheel or sharp knife, cut the dough into 1-inch-wide strips and lightly brush with the egg mixture. You will need 12 strips. Reserve the rolled-out pieces of excess dough.

10. Slice a small piece off of the bottom of each pear so they will stand upright. Pat pears dry with a paper towel. Beginning at the stem end, wrap each pear with slightly overlapping dough strips. You will need 2 strips placed end to end for each pear.

11. Using the reserved dough scraps, take a sharp knife and cut out leaf shapes. Using the dull side of the knife blade, press leaf details into the pastry leaves, if desired. You will need about 3 leaves per pear. Brush the backs of the leaves with the egg mixture and press the leaves onto the pastry around the stem end of each pear. Brush each whole pear again with the egg mixture and place on a baking sheet.

12. Bake the pears for 40 to 45 minutes, or until the pastry is lightly browned. Reheat the reserved port sauce; transfer the pears to serving plates and serve with sauce.

AFTERNOON IN ASPEN

Hungarian Goulash

I tasted this classic version of goulash at the Aspen Mountain Club, and found it to be one of the best come-in-from-the-cold meals ever. I serve it with spaetzle or egg noodles tossed with a little butter and parsley. It is even better made the day before.
Serves 4 to 6

> 3 tablespoons goose fat, duck fat, or olive oil
> 2 onions, coarsely chopped
> 3½ pounds stewing beef, cut into 2-inch cubes
> 2 garlic cloves, chopped
> 1 teaspoon caraway seeds
> 3 tablespoons sweet Hungarian paprika
> 1½ cups dry red wine
> 3 cups beef stock
> 4 whole tomatoes, skinned, seeded, and chopped
> 1 cup sweet gherkins, julienned
> 2 tablespoons sour cream, plus more for serving
> Salt and freshly ground pepper

1. In a large soup pot over medium-high heat, melt the goose fat.
2. Add the onions and sauté until golden; add the beef and sauté until browned.
3. Add the garlic, caraway seeds, and paprika and cook for an additional 5 minutes.
4. Add the wine and cook for 5 minutes. Add the beef stock and cover. Braise for one hour.
5. Add the tomatoes, and continue braising for another hour. The goulash can be made ahead up to this point and refrigerated. The fat will congeal and can be removed easily.

6. Skim the fat and add the gherkins. Season to taste with salt and pepper.
7. In a bowl, stir a little sauce into the sour cream; add that to the goulash. If reheating, do so gently, being careful not to boil. Serve with spaetzle or egg noodles topped with a dollop of sour cream.

VALENTINE'S DAY IN PARIS

Crème Brûlée

Romantic dinners should end with an elegant dessert, and crème brûlée fits the bill, especially when served in heart-shaped ramekins. This recipe creates more than just two—but is a dinner party classic.
Serves 12

> 9 large eggs
> 4 cups heavy cream
> ½ cup sugar
> 1 tablespoon pure vanilla extract
> 1 tablespoon lemon or orange zest
> 2 tablespoons packed light brown sugar

1. Preheat oven to 300°F.
2. Separate the eggs, placing the yolks in a small bowl. (Save the whites for another use.)
3. In a medium saucepan, bring the cream, sugar, vanilla, and lemon zest to a boil. Remove from the heat.
4. Add a tablespoon of the hot cream to the yolks and whisk to combine. Pour the mixture into the pot and whisk.
5. Pour into twelve 4-ounce remekins or custard cups. Place in a small roasting pan and set on the middle oven rack. Carefully pour boiling water into the roasting pan to come halfway up the sides of the ramekins. Bake 1 hour, or until the custards are firm. Carefully remove the pan from the oven and cool on a wire rack. Refrigerate custards at least 3 hours, until well chilled.
6. Preheat the broiler. Press the brown sugar through a sieve over the tops of the chilled custards. Place the ramekins on a jelly-roll pan, and broil 3 minutes, just until sugar melts. Serve within 4 hours, so the sugar crusts remain crisp.

Shrimp Risotto

No matter how many times I serve this delectable dish, guests never tire of it. I think it's partly the spark of the red pepper flakes that awakens the palate—and then again, the butter, fresh shrimp, and grated Parmesan cheese contribute a lot, too. *Serves 6 to 8*

> 5 tablespoons extra virgin olive oil
> 1 teaspoon red pepper flakes
> 2 pounds raw medium shrimp, shelled and deveined
> 1 cup coarsely chopped shallots
> 2 garlic cloves, chopped
> 6 cups chicken stock
> 2 cups Arborio rice
> 1 cup dry white wine
> ½ cup freshly grated Parmesan cheese
> 2 tablespoons butter
> Salt and pepper
> ¼ cup chopped scallions
> ¼ cup chopped parsley

1. Heat 2 tablespoons of the olive oil in a large frying pan over high heat. Add the red pepper flakes and shrimp and sauté just until the shrimp turn pink and are a little underdone. Set aside.
2. Heat the rest of the olive oil in a large saucepan on medium heat. Add the shallots and garlic and sauté until golden. In a saucepan, heat the chicken stock to a simmer.
3. Add the rice to the shallot mixture in the saucepan and stir until it is well coated. Add the wine and cook until it has been absorbed. Add about ½ cup of the simmering broth to the rice, stirring until liquid has been absorbed. Continue cooking over medium-low heat, adding remaining broth ½ cup at a time and stirring after each addition, until all liquid has been absorbed and rice is tender but still firm, about 25 minutes. Rice should have a creamy consistency.
4. When the risotto is cooked, stir in the Parmesan and butter. The rice should be very creamy. Add more liquid if necessary and season with salt and pepper to taste.
5. Fold in the shrimp mixture, scallions, and parsley. Serve immediately.

Coconut Flan

Custards like this delicious flan created by Leila Roxo, a Weatherstone staffer, are baked in a pan of hot water, also known as a bain-marie. The water diffuses the heat of the oven so the flan does not overcook or separate. *Serves 8*

> Two 12-ounce cans condensed milk
> 3 cans whole milk
>   (use the condensed milk can to measure)
> 1 cup sweetened shredded coconut
> 4 large eggs
> 1 tablespoon cornstarch
> 3 cups sugar

1. Preheat the oven to 375°F. Butter a 9-inch springform pan. Bring a kettle of water to a boil.
2. Combine all the ingredients except the sugar in a blender and mix well.
3. Heat the sugar in a medium saucepan oven medium heat, stirring constantly with a wooden spoon until the sugar begins to melt and turn light brown; it will caramelize into a sticky syrup.
4. Pour the caramel into the prepared springform pan. Pour the milk mixture over the caramel. To set up the bain-marie, set the springform pan in a larger metal pan; place in the oven. Carefully pour boiling water into the large baking pan to come halfway up the sides of the springform pan. Bake in the water bath for 40 to 50 minutes.

5 . Remove from the oven, and remove the springform pan from the bain-marie, making sure no water goes into the flan. Cool on a wire rack. Refrigerate in the pan for 3 hours, or until well chilled.

6 . Serve on a chilled platter.

Halibut with Fried Fresh Herbs and Lemon

Any firm white fish will do for this easy dish—but it's absolutely essential to use fresh herbs for standout results.
Serves 4 to 6

> Six 6-ounce halibut fillets or steaks
> ¼ cup extra virgin olive oil
> Salt and freshly ground pepper
> 3 tablespoons chopped fresh thyme
> 3 tablespoons chopped fresh sage
> 3 tablespoons chopped fresh flat-leaf parsley
> 2 tablespoons lemon juice

1 . Preheat the broiler.

2 . Rub the fish with 1 tablespoon of the olive oil, salt, and pepper and broil for 6 to 8 minutes on each side, depending on thickness.

3 . Meanwhile, heat the remaining olive oil in a small frying pan over medium heat. When the oil is hot, add the herbs and cook for 1 minute; add the lemon juice and cook for 1 more minute. Transfer the fish to a serving platter, pour the sauce over the fish, and serve immediately.

Almond Soup

This pure white soup is an indulgence with its use of butter and heavy cream. You can justify serving it to your guests if you focus on the nutritional benefits of the almonds! Plus, it looks—and tastes—like a dream.
Serves 6

> 3 tablespoons unsalted butter
> 1 cup chopped onion
> 3 garlic cloves, chopped
> 1 cup chopped celery
> 1 cup dry white wine
> 1 cup whole blanched almonds, ground
> 3 cups chicken stock
> 1 teaspoon cumin
> 1 cup heavy cream
> Salt and freshly ground pepper
> 3 whole sprigs cilantro

1 . In a soup pot, melt the butter and sauté the onion, garlic, and celery until soft.

2 . Add the wine and simmer for 10 minutes.

3 . Add the almonds, chicken stock, and cumin and simmer another 20 minutes. Let the soup cool slightly.

4 . Puree the soup in a blender. Return it to the pot, add the cream, season to taste with salt and pepper, and simmer for 10 more minutes. Garnish with the cilantro and serve.

Chicken Satay with Peanut Sauce

This Indonesian marinade also works with pork.
Makes 12 skewers

⅓ cup tamari or soy sauce
3 garlic cloves, minced
2 teaspoons finely chopped fresh ginger
1 teaspoon red curry paste
1 cup unsweetened coconut milk
2 tablespoons chopped fresh cilantro
½ cup chicken stock
2 whole boneless, skinless chicken breasts,
    each cut into 6 long strips
Peanut Sauce (recipe follows)

1. Combine all the ingredients except the chicken and Peanut Sauce in a dish large enough to hold the chicken and mix well.

2. Add the chicken and marinate in the refrigerator for 1 to 2 hours.

3. Prepare an outdoor grill or preheat the broiler.

4. Soak twelve 6-inch bamboo skewers in cold water for at least 15 minutes. Remove and pat dry. Thread the chicken loosely on the skewers.

5. Grill or broil for 3 minutes on each side or until completely cooked. Serve hot with Peanut Sauce.

PEANUT SAUCE
Makes 3 cups

1 cup unsweetened coconut milk
¾ cup chunky peanut butter
1 tablespoon red curry paste
3 tablespoons lime juice
3 tablespoons honey
½ cup chicken stock
1 garlic clove, crushed
⅓ cup chopped scallions
¼ cup chopped fresh cilantro

In a saucepan over medium heat, combine all ingredients except the scallions and cilantro, and cook for 5 minutes. Let the sauce cool. Add the scallions and cilantro and stir to combine. When ready to serve, add the scallions and cilantro and stir to combine.

recipe index

photo credits

Cover: Sylvie Becquet.

Title Page, pages 2–3: Sylvie Becquet.

Contents, pages 6–7: Sylvie Becquet.

Spring, page 11: Sylvie Becquet.

June Peony Party, pages 12–23: Sylvie Becquet.

Blooms Day Lunch, pages 24–29: Sylvie Becquet.

Flower Power Fun, pages 30–39: Sylvie Becquet.

Summer, page 40: Sylvie Becquet.

Birthday Bash for the Beaty Girls, pages 42–55: Sylvie Becquet.

The Fourth of July, pages 56–71: Sylvie Becquet.

Sunflower Soirée, pages 72–81: Sylvie Becquet.

Exotic and Enchanting, pages 82–87: Sylvie Becquet.

Autumn, page 88: Sylvie Becquet.

Autumn Barn Dance, pages 90–91: Mick Hales; pages 92–103: Antonis Achilleos.

A Dickens–Inspired Halloween, pages 104–117: Stefan Studer.

The Hunt Ball, pages 118–139: Tara Sgroi.

Holiday Entertaining, page 140: Sylvie Becquet.

'Tis the Season, pages 142–149: Sylvie Becquet.

Christmastime in the City, pages 150–155: Sylvie Becquet.

A Holiday Tradition, pages 156–163: Sylvie Becquet.

Christmas Eve at Weatherpebble, pages 164–169: Sylvie Becquet.

Christmas in Aspen, pages 170–179: Sylvie Becquet.

Winter, page 180: Sylvie Becquet.

Winter Wonderland, pages 182–187: Sylvie Becquet.

Valentine's Day in Paris, pages 188–191: Sylvie Becquet.

Bridal Shower Lunch, pages 192–197: Carolyne Roehm.

Raise the Red Lanterns! page 198–213: Sylvie Becquet.

Afternoon in Aspen, pages 214–227: Alan Becker.

BROADWAY

PUBLISHED BY BROADWAY BOOKS

Published in the United States by Broadway Books, an imprint
of The Doubleday Broadway Publishing Group, a division of
Random House, Inc., New York.
www.broadwaybooks.com

BROADWAY BOOKS and its logo, a letter B bisected on the
diagonal, are trademarks of Random House, Inc.

Book design by Doug Turshen with David Huang

Some photographs in this book have previously appeared in
Veranda and *House Beautiful* magazines.

The cataloging-in-publication data is on file with
the Library of Congress.

ISBN-13: 978-0-7679-2523-5
ISBN-10: 0-7679-2523-8

PRINTED IN CHINA
10 9 8 7 6 5 4 3 2

First Edition